THE ORIGINS AND DEVELOPMENT OF
CLASSICAL HINDUISM

A. L. BASHAM

THE ORIGINS AND DEVELOPMENT OF CLASSICAL HINDUISM

EDITED AND COMPLETED
BY KENNETH G. ZYSK

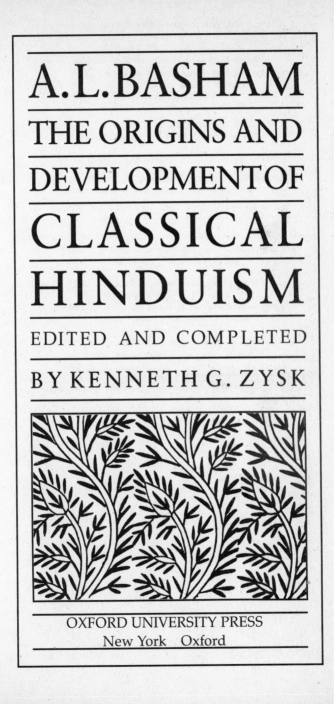

OXFORD UNIVERSITY PRESS
New York Oxford

Oxford University Press

Oxford New York Toronto
Delhi Bombay Calcutta Madras Karachi
Petaling Jaya Singapore Hong Kong Tokyo
Nairobi Dar es Salaam Cape Town
Melbourne Auckland
and associated companies in
Berlin Ibadan

First published in 1989 by Beacon Press

First issued as an Oxford University Press paperback, 1991
Published by arrangement with Beacon Press

Library of Congress Cataloging-in-Publication Data
Basham, A. L. (Arthur Llewellyn)
The origins and development of classical Hinduism / A.L. Basham ; edited and completed by Kenneth G. Zysk.
p. cm.
Reprint. Originally published: Boston : Beacon Press, c1989.
Includes bibliographical references and index.
1. Hinduism—History. I. Zysk, Kenneth G. II. Title.
[BL1152.3.B37 1991]
294.5'09'01—dc20 *91-18884*
CIP

ISBN 0-19-507349-5 (PBK.)

2 4 6 8 10 9 7 5 3 1

Printed in the United States of America

Contents

List of Illustrations

Acknowledgments

The project of editing, annotating, and completing for publication A. L. Basham's lectures on the origin and development of classical Hinduism came into my hands shortly after his death, in 1986. Professor Willard Oxtoby of the University of Toronto, then president of the Religious Studies Section of the American Council of Learned Societies, gave me the lectures, which he had already typed on to computer diskette. I am grateful to Professor Oxtoby for providing me copies of those diskettes.

Shortly after learning about the project, Professor James A. Santucci of California State University at Fullerton, a former student of Basham's, offered to supply the illustrations that were part of an exhibition on Hindu art in South and Southeast Asia which he organized at his institution in 1986. They are published for the first time in this work. I am deeply appreciative to Professor Santucci for the use of this extraordinary collection of Hindu art and for his catalogue of the collection, from which the captions derive. I am also grateful to Professor Thomas Trautmann of the University of Michigan, another student of Basham's, for valuable comments he made on my contributions.

Throughout the preparation of the work, Dr. Namita Basham, A. L.'s widow, who now resides in Shillong, Assam, India, has been supportive of the project and has provided useful biographical information about her late husband. Her strength during the trying time after Basham's death is to be admired. I sincerely appreciate all the support and information she has given to me.

Finally, I should like to thank Dr. Adriana Berger for compiling the index and, at Beacon Press, the editor, Deborah Johnson, her assistant, Deborah Chasman, Thomas Fischer, managing editor, and the design and production manager, Pam Pokorney, as well as all those on the staff who helped to produce such a beautiful book.

Kenneth G. Zysk

Introduction

Hinduism is the major religious tradition of the subcontinent of South Asia. Its adherents in India number well over three hundred million. Like all the major religions of the world, Hinduism has spread beyond the borders of its homeland, originally to Southeast Asia and more recently to the Western world, where numerous neo-Hindu movements have found fertile ground. This book is a history of the development of Hinduism from earliest times to the early centuries of the common era, written by one of the world's leading scholars of ancient Indian cultural history, A. L. Basham.

Hinduism has gone through several stages in its evolution, and certain terms have been developed and used by Western and Indian scholars alike to distinguish one stage from another. Throughout this work the terms *Brāhmaṇism* and *Hinduism* will be encountered. A fundamental distinction between them should be borne in mind: Brāhmaṇism applies to the religion of the earliest periods and is generally synonymous with Vedism; Hinduism refers to the entire stream of the orthodox religion of the subcontinent, from (and sometimes including) the Vedic period to the present. According to Basham, the relationship of

Brāhmaṇism to Hinduism is "similar to that between the sacrificial Judaism of the temple and the later Judaism of the synagogue."[1]

One encounters a vocabulary dominated by the masculine gender during all stages in the development of classical Hinduism. This is not the case because of the author's preference but rather because religious literature was composed entirely by priests and sages for the exclusive use of men of the higher socio-religious orders. Only after the classical period did Hinduism begin to give significant attention to women. This corresponded, as we shall see in the last chapter, with the beginning of worship of female divinities whose names, of course, occur in the feminine gender in the scriptures.

The book is based on a series of five lectures given on ten key university campuses in the United States during the autumn, winter, and spring of 1984–85. They were the last public lectures in North America presented by A. L. Basham before his death, in January 1986, and represent the synthesis of a lifetime of study and reflection on the origins and development of Hinduism.

Modelled on his monumental work *The Wonder That Was India,* first published in 1954 and reprinted numerous times since then, the chapters in this book offer the reader a clear and lucid account of the evolution of classical Hinduism. Basham incorporates new insights into his discussion of the development of Hinduism, resulting in a clearly presented and mature interpretation of the growth of one of the world's major religious traditions. The presentation of information is historical rather than thematic, focusing on an analysis of texts as well as archaeological and art-historical data. Written with the general reader in mind, the book answers many of the questions undergraduate students often ask; yet the advanced student will also benefit from the author's vast knowledge of the subject. The chapters of the book were originally offered as five public lectures under the following titles: "The *Ṛg-veda* and the Beginnings of Philosophy," "The Development of Sacrificial Religion in the Later Vedic Literature," "The Origins of the Doctrine of Transmigration," "The Growth of Mysticism and the Upaniṣads," and "The Rise of Theism and the Composition of the *Bhagavad-gītā*."[2]

The first chapter begins with an examination of the prehistorical religion of South Asia, which dates from about 2700 to 1700 B.C.E. It is based principally on informed speculations from archaeological reports. This is followed by a presentation of the religion of the early Vedic period (about 1500–900 B.C.E.), which offers a stimulating analysis of the sacrificial tradition and the cult of divinities, utilizing the *Ṛg-veda,* the most sacred of Hindu scriptures, as principal source material.

Chapter 2 uses the latest, or tenth, book of the *Ṛg-veda* and the *Atharva-veda,* a somewhat later Vedic text, to launch into a discussion of Hinduism's attempts to explain the origin of the world. This is followed by a general analysis of later Vedic literature (about 900–500 B.C.E.) and its contents and concludes with a discussion of the Vedic sacrificial system.

Chapter 3 focuses on the further development of Hindu philosophical thought in the speculative literature of the Āraṇyakas and Upaniṣads, which make up part of the later Vedic literature. This chapter contains the author's unique analysis of the origin of the doctrine of transmigration. Basham radically departs from the existing theories, which suggest that the doctrine derived from the indigenous non-Hindu traditions of ancient India. He offers strong evidence that the notion of transmigration was an esoteric doctrine, developed among certain circles of orthodox Hindus.

Chapter 4 examines the evolution of the mystic traditions beginning with the orthodox asceticism of the early Upaniṣads and continues with a brief survey of the principal heterodox ascetic traditions of Buddhists, Jains, and Ājīvikas (from about the sixth to the fourth centuries B.C.E.). The author maintains that the heterodox forms of asceticism and mysticism derived from the orthodox forms.

Chapter 5 discusses the historical background and development of the epic tradition in South Asia and focuses on the composition and contents of the *Mahābhārata,* the story of the rivalry and war between two ruling families, the Pāṇḍavas and the Kauravas, and the *Rāmāyaṇa,* the story of Rāma. The dates of these two epics are much debated. The *Mahābhārata* probably goes back to about 900 B.C.E., but was finally edited around 500 C.E., by which time the *Rāmāyaṇa* was already well known.

Chapter 6 addresses the *Bhagavad-gītā,* its place in the epic tradition and its religious significance, and the rise of theism. The author marshals strong and original evidence that the *Bhagavad-gītā,* the Hindu equivalent of the Christian New Testament, is in fact a composite of three different strata written by at least three authors over a period of about two hundred years, reaching its final form around 100 B.C.E. Each of the three authors added a new religious doctrine, forming in the end a text epitomizing the new orthodoxy of classical Hinduism. (Chapters 5 and 6 are based on Basham's fifth lecture.)

The final chapter contains the editor's concluding remarks. Previous chapters make only passing references to the manuals on Vedic lore (*Kalpa Sūtras*) and the literature pertaining to the duties of a Hindu (*dharma*). The former date from about the sixth to the third centuries B.C.E., while the core writings of the latter range from the third century B.C.E. to the early centuries C.E. As these texts are crucial for the proper understanding of Hinduism, the editor has provided a brief survey of this material, along with a few remarks on the development of Hinduism to the present day, emphasizing the movements that have flourished in the West. The intent in this chapter is not to be comprehensive but rather to sketch out the development of Hinduism after the classical period, which culminated with the

Bhagavad-gītā, and to illustrate its adaptability in the face of internal and external influences.

There is an appendix of Basham's publications on ancient Indian history and culture for those interested in his thought. The bibliography has been compiled to help readers deepen their understanding of Hinduism. It includes general materials for beginners as well as sources for more advanced students.

The attractiveness of this study is supplemented by numerous illustrations of Hindu art never before published. The artefacts come from several private collections in California, and most were analyzed, identified, and catalogued by Professor James A. Santucci of California State University at Fullerton. He was also responsible for the production of the fine prints.

Since the lectures were not prepared for publication before the author's death, this has been the major task of the editor. The main body of the text remains virtually as it was delivered, with citations added, factual errors corrected, and stylistic changes made to reflect a written rather than oral presentation.

As this book represents the final major contribution of A. L. Basham, it is appropriate to offer the reader a brief biography of the author. (The appendix contains a list of his principal publications.) Arthur Llewellyn Basham, or "Bash," as he was fondly called by his friends and colleagues, was born on the 24th of May, 1914, in Laughton, Essex, England. His father, Edward Arthur Abraham Basham, was a free-lance journalist who served in the Indian army at Kasauli (near Simla) as a volunteer during World War I. Young Arthur learned about the wonders of India from the exciting accounts of his father, who taught him to count in Hindustānī (nowadays known as Hindī-Urdū). His mother, Maria Jane Basham, also a journalist and an accomplished short story writer, instilled her son with a love of language and literature and a deep appreciation of religion. Basham inherited from his parents precisely those qualities which would distinguish him as the foremost elucidator of ancient Indian history and culture in recent decades.

Basham was not only a master of *lettres* but also an accomplished musician. At the age of seven he began learning to play the piano. His instructor not only taught conventional sight reading and finger techniques but also filled his pupil with an appreciation and love of music. By the age of sixteen, Arthur had written several compositions of his own. In later years, on visits to the Bashams' home, students and friends might be entertained by selections from Mozart's piano concertos or from Schubert's piano sonatas.

During his formative years, A. L. Basham tried his hand at writing and even published a collection of poems, *Proem* (London, 1935), and a novel, *Golden Furrow* (London, 1939). He quickly realized, however, that his real calling lay in the study of ancient Indian history and culture. He won an Ouseley Scholarship to study Oriental languages at the London School of Oriental and African Studies and in 1941 graduated with first-class honours in Indo-Aryan Studies from that institution. During the turbulent years of World War II, Basham was a conscientious objector. Until the end of the war, he pursued his studies independently, while serving as a fireman in the Auxiliary Fire Service at Lowestoft. After the war, he reentered the School of Oriental and African Studies to pursue advanced studies in Indology under the supervision of L. D. Barnett, a distinguished British Scholar of ancient Indian history and culture. He completed his Ph.D. in 1951, with a thesis that has become the classic study of a forgotten ancient Indian religion, *The History and Doctrines of the Ājīvikas,* which was published the following year. This book, which brought together all the available information on the sixth-century B.C.E. religious sect of the Ājīvikas, opened the door for a more complete understanding of the ascetic traditions of ancient India. It remains a principal source book in the history of Indian religions.

Already in 1948, Basham had been appointed lecturer in the history of India at the School of Oriental and African Studies, and he rose to the rank of reader in 1953 and professor in the history of South Asia in 1957. He served in this capacity until 1965, when he was called to Australia to become professor and head of the Department of Asian Civilisations at the Australian National University in Canberra. He remained at this post until his retirement, in 1979. In 1965, Basham had been awarded an honorary D.Litt. from Kurukshetra University. The following year he was given a D.Litt. by the University of London for his work on the history of South Asia; and in 1977, he received an honorary D.Litt. (Vidyā-vāridhi, or Ocean of knowledge) from Nava Nālandā Mahāvihāra (Buddhist Studies Research Institute), Bihār, India. He travelled and lectured extensively during his career and held numerous visiting professorships in South Asia and in North and South America both before and after his retirement. He held his final post for about six months. In September 1985, he was appointed Swāmī Vivekānanda Professor in Oriental Studies at the Asiatic Society in Calcutta. He died of cancer in Calcutta on 27 January 1986 and was buried two days later in Old Military Cemetery of All Saints Cathedral, Shillong, Meghālaya, India, not far from the home of his wife, Namita Catherine, his son, Ashok James, and his daughter, Maria Sāvitrī.

As a keen promoter of Oriental studies, Basham had been elected a fellow of many learned societies in Britain, Australia, and India and distinguished himself as an active administrator and organizer. He was director of the Royal Asiatic Society of Great Britain and Ireland from 1964 to 1965 and president of the 28th International Congress of Orientalists when it met in Canberra, Australia, in 1971. He was instrumental in organizing the first International Conference on the Study of Traditional Asian Medicine in 1979 and was elected the first president of the Society for the Study of Traditional Asian Medicine, which today boasts branches on most of the seven continents. He also served as president of the International Association of Buddhist Studies from 1981 to 1985.

In spite of his travels, lectures, and committee appointments, Basham was also able to make original contributions to South Asian studies through his publications. His major work was *The Wonder That Was India,* with which nearly every student of South Asia is familiar. It remains one of the best and most comprehensive surveys of the culture of the Indian subcontinent prior to the coming of the Muslims in the tenth century C.E. A masterpiece of synthesis, this textbook has the singular quality of bringing ancient India to life through the author's recognition of India's past accomplishments. Basham's clear and lucid prose has made ancient Indian history and culture accessible to a wide audience.

Perhaps Basham's greatest work was to have been a history of the Gypsies, or Romanies, with whom he had had a fascination since his days as a youth in Essex. He often lectured on the Gypsies and occasionally made references to them in his published work. In the end, time did not permit him to write the book.

Basham's writings might have been more numerous had he not been the teacher that he was. He was very much a *guru* in the Indian sense. As such, the knowledge he transmitted was passed on orally, especially to his graduate and research students, of whom he had over a hundred. He often stated publicly that his greatest contributions to Indian studies were his students, many of whom have gone on to become distinguished scholars in their respective fields of South Asian studies. This remarkable man, through the enthusiasm he brought to the subject, tried to instill the same excitement in those he taught. More often than not he succeeded.

Basham's approach to the study of Indian religions and Hinduism in particular may be characterized as traditional Indology with personal intuition, for it combined history, philology, and phenomenology.[3] In *The Wonder That Was India,* he describes his approach to the study of ancient Indian history as follows: "The early history of India resembles a jigsaw puzzle with many missing pieces; some parts of the picture are fairly clear, others may be reconstructed with the aid of a controlled imagination" (44). We can replace "The early history of India" with "The origins and development of classical Hinduism" to obtain a clear statement of Basham's methodology in the lectures on which this book is based. His "controlled imagination" came very close to a type of phenomenological approach. The hard data, in the form of textual references, archaeological artefacts, and art-historical and numismatic evidence, represented the pieces of a jigsaw puzzle. It was the scholar's task to put these pieces together to present a coherent picture. The principal rule of the game, however, was that one must not deviate from the data presented; in other words, all the pieces must fit together without being forced. It was incumbent on the scholar to discover the larger picture of which the fragmentary data were the parts, thus revealing its significance. Philology and comparative history, religion and literature were the scholar's principal tools. Personal experience and intuition were not excluded as long as they did not contradict existing hard data. When properly executed, this process of "controlled imagination" would produce a reasonably accurate picture of ancient Indian history or of Hinduism. Since data derived from ancient India are notorious for being ahistorical and generally wanting in any sense of chronology, an exact picture is hardly attainable.

Throughout his career, Basham never deviated from his fundamental approach to Indian history and culture. But he did refine and synthesize it based on new information derived from the research of students, extensive reading, and frequent trips to India. This presentation of the origins and development of classical Hinduism is the product of his many years of refinement and synthesis.

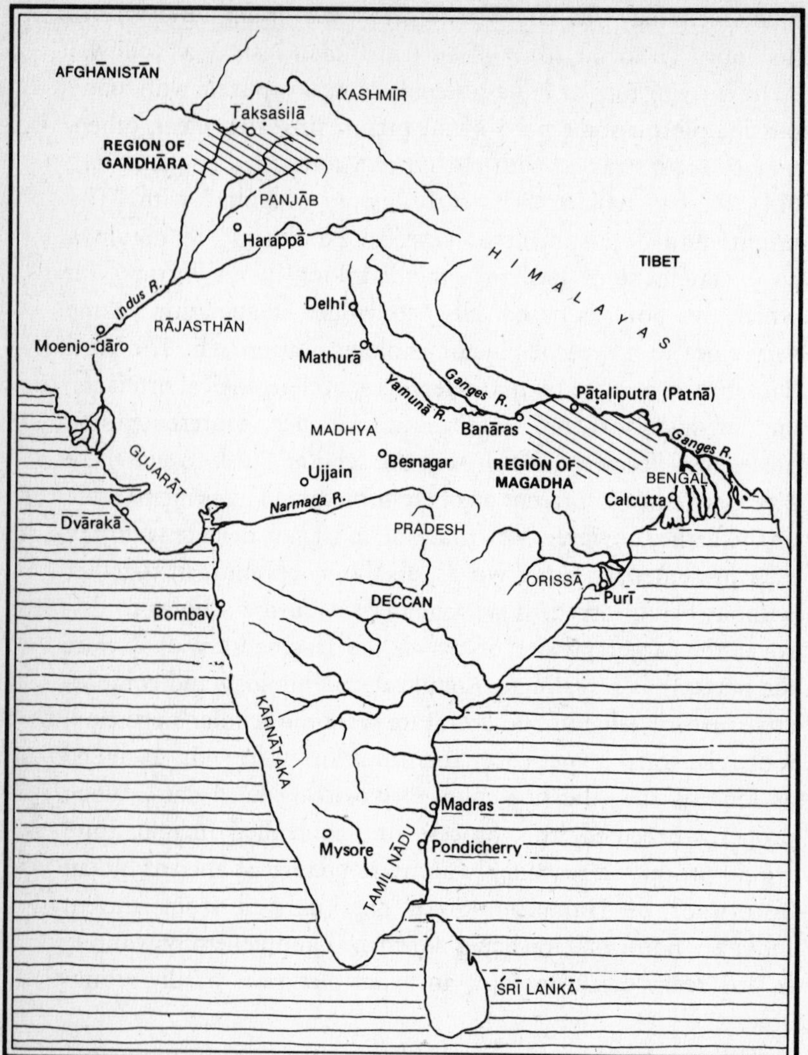
AFGHĀNISTĀN
KASHMĪR
Taksaśilā
REGION OF GANDHĀRA
PANJĀB
Harappā
HIMALAYAS
TIBET
Indus R.
RĀJASTHĀN
Moenjo-dāro
Delhī
Mathurā
Ganges R.
Yamunā R.
Pātaliputra (Patnā)
Banāras
MADHYA
GUJARĀT
Besnagar
Ujjain
REGION OF MAGADHA
Ganges R.
BENGAL
Calcutta
Narmada R.
Dvārakā
PRADESH
ORISSĀ
Purī
DECCAN
Bombay
KĀRNĀTAKA
Madras
Mysore
Pondicherry
TAMIL NĀDU
ŚRĪ LAṄKĀ

THE ORIGINS AND DEVELOPMENT OF

CLASSICAL HINDUISM

ONE

The Beginnings of Religion in South Asia

Prehistoric Religion in South Asia

Agriculture, based on information from archaeologists and carbon-14 dating, began in South Asia around 5000 B.C.E., in small settlements of neolithic peasants and stock breeders in what is now Pakistān. By 3000 B.C.E. much of the Indus valley was cultivated, and bronze was beginning to be used for practical purposes. The culture was by no means uniform: Wide differences are found in the pottery from village to village, and other features of daily life show comparable variation. Most of the village cultures, however, were by comparison well advanced, and though they had not yet evolved a civilization, in the sense of a literate city life, they were well on the way to doing so.

Out of the village cultures there began to crystallize, in about 2700 B.C.E., a great civilization. This, known to archaeologists as the Harappā culture and more popularly referred to as the Indus civilization, seems to have developed on the soil of the subcontinent and was not brought to India by invaders.

Its main centres were two large cities, the original names of which are unknown to us. They are now known by the names of the modern villages nearest the sites, Moenjo-dāro[1] and Harappā. Moenjo-dāro, on the right bank of the Indus River below the great Sukkur dam, is about 400 to 500 miles (650 to 800 kilometres) from Harappā, which is on the Rāvī River about 100 to 150 miles (160 to 240 kilometres) from Lahore, the chief city of the Pakistāni Panjāb. Besides these two great cities there were numerous smaller ones, and village sites of the Harappā culture have been found as far afield as Gujarāt in the southeast, along the Makrān coast in the southwest, and the Gomal valley in the northwest. Traces of its contact have been found farther afield, in Soviet Central Asia and even in Mesopotamia itself.

The two large cities of this great culture bear such a similarity to each other that it seems clear they were closely linked, probably politically as well as culturally; we cannot yet read the script of the Indus civilization, and thus we can only guess at the way the cities were governed.

Early in the second millennium B.C.E. there were great geological changes that badly affected the cities, especially Moenjo-dāro. A sudden rise in the level of the sea bed south of the delta of the Indus slowed down the course of the river, with the result that the city, always liable to inundation, was more frequently and more seriously flooded. Probably the waterlogged soil became less productive. There are clear signs of the decline of city life in Moenjo-dāro and of overpopulation, probably caused by an influx of refugees, many from villages whose land could no longer support all the inhabitants. Finally, it seems, Moenjo-dāro was abandoned by all but a few families. A raid by outsiders, who may have been Āryans from the west, resulted in the slaughter of a considerable number of these people, and then the city was deserted almost completely. This probably took place about 1700 B.C.E., after which the inundated city was slowly converted by the elements into a series of high mounds, where only occasional bricks and sherds of pottery coming to the surface of the soil indicated its former greatness. Nearly two thousand years after the city's abandonment a Buddhist *stūpa*[2] was erected on top of the highest mound, called by the local Sindī peasants *Moen-jo-dāro,* the Mound of the Dead. Later this *stūpa* too was abandoned, when the local Buddhists embraced the new religion of Islām. Eventually it became a place of awe and fear among the people who lived in its shadow. Only in the 1920s was its importance realized and the great city excavated by a British team led by Sir John Marshall.

The northern city, near the modern village of Harappā, had a different fate. This was for a while in part occupied by invaders with horses, animals virtually unknown to the indigenous people at that time. The identity of these newcomers is unknown, but most authorities speculate that they were Āryans. Later these migrants seem to have abandoned Harappā, but its final fate is not very clear, since the bricks of which it was built were removed in enormous numbers in the nineteenth century to lay the bed of a nearby railway line.

Without written records of this prehistoric civilization, our knowledge of its religion is very defective, but we may be sure that it had certain features common to both the ancient religions of the Middle East and the later religion of India. Noteworthy is the evidence of the many seals found in the sites, which show that the bull was a sacred animal. Moreover the sites have yielded many terra-cotta figurines of broad-hipped women, some with fantastic headdresses, which were evidently representations of a goddess. These features, the Mother Goddess representing the Earth and the sacred bull representing the fertilizing sky, were common to early agriculturists throughout Euro-Asia. They are the main elements of a cult designed to insure the fertility of crops, herds, and humans.

We can also be fairly certain that the religion of the Harappā culture emphasized ritual purity, maintained by ablution with water. This is proved by the presence of a drained bathroom in almost every house and by the large "swimming pool," surrounded by small cells, in Moenjo-dāro. It is very unlikely that the purpose of these was purely hygienic. It was probably felt that washing and bathing were absolutely necessary to preserve the purity without which one's body would become the prey of evil spirits.

It is also obvious that the people of the Indus believed in some kind of survival after death, for they buried their dead, unlike later Indians, who practised cremation. With the dead were buried pots, which originally no doubt contained food for the afterlife. (Elaborate funerals with many grave goods, such as occurred in ancient Egypt and sporadically in Sumer, are not attested.)

The features of the Indus religion just outlined are fairly certain. Other features, mainly gathered from seals, are the horned god (who appears on one or two seals) and the *pīpal* tree, with its spear-shaped leaves, which is depicted in numerous contexts and which must have been sacred, as it was sacred in later times in both Buddhism and Hinduism.

The horned god appears to be ithyphallic; it is generally accepted that he has traces of two faces in profile, as well as that facing the observer; he is surrounded by animals—an elephant, a rhinoceros, a buffalo, a tiger, a long-horned goat—and his lcgs are bent in a difficult posture, with the soles of the feet pressed together, known to later yogins as *utkaṭikāsana*. These facts have led to his identification as the prototype of the later Hindu god Śiva, and it is often confidently stated that the religion of the Harappā culture was an early form of Hinduism. The evidence, in our view, is inadequate. The identification of two profile faces is very uncertain (they may be parts of the god's headdress); the full face of the god is closer to that of a tiger than that of a man; it is not completely certain that the god is ithyphallic, since the marks taken to indicate this may be merely the loose part of a girdle; most of the animals associated with the god are not those specially connected with Śiva. In fact the evidence for any kind of continuity between this prehistoric god and Śiva is rather weak.[3]

Evidence for other features of Hinduism in the civilization of the Indus is even more dubious. It has been suggested that this culture practised ritual prostitution, in the manner of the temple prostitution of later India, or that the inducement of trance or calm states, later called yoga, was practised. But the evidence for these practices is so tenuous that the suggestions are quite unacceptable except as faint possibilities.

An enigmatic feature of the ancient cities of the Indus is that nowhere in them is found a building that can be confidently identified as a temple, though there are one or two large halls that may have served this purpose. No monumental statuary, no traces of mural painting have been discovered. It seems that the main focus of the religious life of the people was the home—a feature that is still fundamentally true of Indian religion. Jews, Christians, or Muslims must, if they wish to be considered pious members of their faiths, attend their places of worship at regular intervals. On the other hand, it is possible to be a very devout Hindu without ever going near the temple, which is a late development in Hinduism and is still not one of its essential features.

If we know very little about the religion of the Indus, we know even less about the prehistoric religion of other areas of the subcontinent. Excavations in many parts of India have yielded well-made pottery and tools of stone and bronze from the third, second, and early first millenniums B.C.E., with iron beginning to appear from about 1000 B.C.E. Only in a few sites have remains been found which throw significant light on the religious life of the times.

Two important sites in the Deccan are worth mentioning. At Daimabād, about fifty miles (eighty kilometres) inland from Bombay, archaeologists excavated a site which produced from a level carbon-dated about 1200 B.C.E. a heavy bronze image of an ithyphallic male figure driving an ox chariot, together with fine bronze figures of a bull, an elephant, and a rhinoceros. Stylistically, these images show clear traces of the influence of the

Indus valley civilization. The people of Daimabād decorated the pottery with friezes of canines, whether wolves or dogs, but this is not sufficient evidence to prove that they held them sacred. They were certainly not sacred in later Hinduism.

Farther inland, at Piklihal, about 300 miles (480 kilometres) south of Bombay in the modern state of Kārnātaka, from about the same period comes evidence of a community of cattle herdsmen who kept their enormous herds in large communal pens and who decorated the rocks in the vicinity of the settlement with innumerable paintings and scratchings of cattle. The diffusion of people such as those of Piklihal may be one of the main sources of the widespread cult of sacred cattle (especially cows) in later Hinduism.

A further interesting feature that developed in the prehistoric religious life of the subcontinent was the introduction of the practice of megalith building. Megaliths, linked up with similar structures in the Middle East and Southeast Asia, appear in Tamil Nādu and parts of eastern India from about the middle of the first millennium B.C.E. They were used as tombs for the interment of the dead, ossuaries for the cremated remains of the members of a family, and memorials. Megaliths were erected by some tribal peoples in out-of-the-way corners of India until quite recent times, but the megalith cult seems never to have affected mainstream religious life in India.

The Āryans and Their Religion

When Europeans first began to take an interest in the religion of India, some of them were told of very ancient texts called Vedas which were so sacred that they were rarely if ever written but were handed down orally from one generation of brāhmaṇs to another. It was only with great difficulty that a few brāhmaṇs in Calcutta were persuaded in the 1780s to divulge the oldest of these texts, the *Ṛg-veda,* but once the text was made public other brāhmaṇs from other parts of India followed them. When versions had been collected from all over the land it was found, to the great surprise of Western scholars, that the text as transmitted in Kashmīr was scarcely different from that transmitted in Tamil Nādu. The *Ṛg-veda* had been passed on orally for nearly three thousand years, with hardly an error. Yet most of the brāhmaṇs who had memorized it had only the very vaguest notions of its meaning, because its language is so archaic that it is almost unintelligible to one trained only in classical Sanskrit. It is rather as though modern English speakers had memorized some mediaeval text like the *Vision of Piers the Plowman* without any real training in the grammar and vocabulary of fourteenth-century English. Perhaps the fact that the *Ṛg-veda* was so imperfectly understood helped to preserve the purity of its transmission.

There are four texts known as Vedas, of which the *Ṛg-veda* is the oldest, having been composed between 1500 and 900 B.C.E. Somewhat later are the *Yajur-veda,* the *Sāma-veda,* and the *Atharva-veda.* The *Ṛg-veda,* the most important from the historian's point of view, is a collection of 1,028 hymns addressed to various gods and intended to be chanted at sacrifices where a hallucinogenic beverage, soma, was made and drunk. The authors of the hymns were certainly not the inhabitants of the ancient Indus cities, for they make no mention of such cities, except possible references to them as having existed in the distant past and having been destroyed. On the other hand, the Vedic hymns frequently mention horses, which did not exist in the Indus cities. While the Indus people knew the tiger, no such mention of this feline occurs in the Vedic hymns. They do, however, speak of the lion (*siṅgha*), which was unknown in the Harappā civilization.

Those who composed and sang the hymns were priests and sages of a people or group of peoples who called themselves

Āryaḥ (anglicized as Āryans) and who entered India when the Indus cities were already half deserted.

We have little archaeological evidence of the Āryans in the first phases of their migration into India, but it is certain that they were akin to similar peoples who were moving into Western Europe at about the same time, bringing horses and chariots and the ancestral forms of the Indo-European languages now spoken in Europe. The ancestors of the Indian Āryans had remained for a long time on the borders of the subcontinent, in what are now Afghānistān and Soviet Central Asia. Some time after the Āryan migration into India, another branch, the ancestors of the Medes and the Persians, left their homeland for what is now Irān and gave their name to that land (the name *Irān* comes from *Airyānām vaējō*, "Realm of the Āryans"). Other Āryans made their presence felt elsewhere in the Middle East. Their culture was not, in some ways, very advanced. They were illiterate and did not live in cities. But they had definite technological advantages over the earlier inhabitants of the Indus valley in their horses and chariots, which are described in great detail in the *Ṛg-veda*, and in their superior metallurgy. Their entry into India took place not as a concerted invasion but in successive waves over several centuries in the earlier half of the second millennium B.C.E. It was when they had settled in the Panjāb that their seers (*ṛṣi*) began to compose the many hymns that were later collected in the *Ṛg-veda*.

The *Ṛg-veda* is divided into ten sections, or books, called in Sanskrit cycles (*maṇḍalas*), of varying length. Internal evidence indicates that the second to seventh books, each composed by sages of separate families, form the oldest stratum; later come the hymns of books eight, nine, one, and ten, in that order, though there is probably much overlapping. It is certain, however, from language, style, and content, that many of the hymns of book ten were composed centuries later than some of those of the earliest books.

The hymns vary widely in style and content. Most of them are in praise of gods, the most popular of whom is Indra, god of war and weather, who has about 250 hymns in his honour, followed by Agni, the fire god, with approximately 200 hymns. Several hymns, however, are not addressed to gods at all. There is one hymn, mostly lost, celebrating the marriage of Sūryā, daughter of the sun god, verses of which are still recited at orthodox Hindu weddings. One or two hymns are for use at funeral rites. There are strange riddle hymns. Other hymns are apparently more or less secular, such as a hymn addressed to the frogs that croak in the rainy season, apparently a rainmaking charm, and the touching lament of a ruined gambler (the Āryans were fond of gambling). Some hymns are in dialogue form, referring to legends, the details of which have long been lost. There are also triumph hymns, celebrating the victory of a certain king named Sudās over a coalition of his enemies. Indeed, though there is a certain sameness about the *Ṛg-veda,* there is also much variety, and the reader who tackles the whole volume is rewarded by many unexpected beauties and stirring passages among the rather repetitive verses of the hymns.

The pandits[4] who transmitted the *Ṛg-veda* preserved its sound with scrupulous accuracy, but they forgot much of its sense. The standard commentary of Sāyaṇa, written in the fourteenth century, shows that much of the original meaning had been forgotten. The earliest gloss on the *Ṛg-veda,* that of Yāska, generally dated in the sixth century B.C.E., shows that even then there were doubts about the meanings of many words. Very few traditional pandits of older times, though they remembered the *Ṛg-veda* perfectly, had more than a vague notion of what it meant. This was not important, however. From the point of view of tradition the hymns of the *Ṛg-veda* have existed from all eternity. The seers did not compose them: they "saw" them; they were inspired to transmit everlasting utterances of enormous spiritual power. Their meaning is not significant—it is the holy sound that counts. For this reason, according to tradition, these hymns are never to be taught to or learned by a woman or a member of the lower orders of society, a *śūdra,* and according to the law book of Manu, if a *śūdra* hears the Veda being recited, his ears are to be filled with molten lead. (We have no positive evidence, incidentally, that this drastic punishment was ever inflicted.)

Though they form the oldest religious literature of India, the hymns of the *Ṛg-veda* are in no way archaic or primitive. They were composed according to strict metrical schemes by sophisticated priests with already developed conventions of poetics and a theology that, if varied and sometimes apparently self-contradictory, was far removed from the simple nature worship attributed by some earlier scholars to primitive humans. The nineteenth-century scholar who produced the standard edition of the *Ṛg-veda,* Max Müller, tried to give his readers, in many of his writings, this false impression of the *Ṛg-veda.* In fact, the Āryans were tough nomads and seminomads with a comparatively advanced technology, an elaborate sacrificial religion, and a class of priestly seers who were the mentors of the tribesmen and also wielded much power through their manipulation of the sacred.

The *Ṛg-veda* was never a popular text. It was composed by and for the religious aristocracy of an intrusive race who had entered India some time earlier and were expanding at the expense of the indigenous inhabitants, of whom some were pushed eastward and southward by the invaders and others were incorporated as second-class citizens in the tribal society. The Āryans were still partly nomadic, at least at the time of the composition of the earlier hymns, interested more in stock breeding than in agriculture. They lived in small villages of kinspeople, and no reference is found anywhere in the *Ṛg-veda* to a town or city.

The hymns are addressed to a pantheon of gods with no very definite hierarchy. It seems that whatever god was being praised at the time was treated as though he was the greatest god of all.

This was a form of religion which Max Müller called henotheism.[5]

Most of the gods were connected with heaven, light, and fire opposed to them were the demons, the spirits of darkness and chaos, whose headquarters were under the earth but who ranged through earth and mid-space, seeking to undo the work of the gods or to injure their worshippers. This dualism of light and darkness, good and evil, order and chaos, was well known to the kindred Irānians and was made by their prophet Zarathuštra (called by the Greeks Zoroaster) the very basis of his system. In India the ancient traditions of cosmic conflict, perhaps an Indo-European inheritance, were never taken so far as in Irān, but from that day to this the strife between the gods and the demons has played an important part in Hindu mythology and in the beliefs of the masses.

Each of the gods had a specific function (*vrata,* which later came to mean vow), which was carried out unfailingly. The gods followed *ṛta,* the cosmic order, the straightforward and regular course of nature. The demons, on the other hand, practised *anṛta,* non-*ṛta;* they tried to overturn the system of nature. (The term *ṛta* almost disappeared in later Sanskrit, giving way to the concept of *dharma,* but *anṛta* remained in use, in the sense of falsehood or unrighteousness.)

Among the gods of the *Ṛg-veda* some were already losing their importance when the hymns were composed. One such was Dyaus, the god of the overarching heaven, to whom only four hymns are addressed. He is interesting because his name is cognate with that of Zeus, the high god of the Greek pantheon, and it is also found in the *Ju-* of the Roman god Jupiter, and in the Germanic war god Tiw, who gave his name to Tuesday. This Dyaus was probably a vestigial form of the high god of the Indo-European-speaking peoples before their tribes were divided.

In many of the earlier hymns of the *Ṛg-veda,* Varuṇa appears as the chief god. He sits in a fine hall or palace in heaven, from which he watches the world below with the help of his spies (*spaś*), who travel throughout the cosmos and bring back news to him. He punishes sinners, first with disease and then with incarceration in the House of Clay, which seems to have had much in common with the Hades of the Greeks and the Sheol of the Jews—a gloomy, cavernous place below the earth, where the shades of the dead remain in a kind of half-life for an indefinite period or forever. Another of Varuṇa's functions is to act as guardian of the *ṛta,* which seems to have been thought of as a principle behind and prior to even the gods.

It is surprising that the Āryans, who at this time had never organized a settled kingdom or lived in a city, should have conceived of a god like Varuṇa, the heavenly emperor in his glorious palace, with innumerable messengers flying through the cosmos at his bidding. Perhaps they had already heard of the mighty kings of Babylonia and modelled Varuṇa on what they had heard and imagined about these kings. Varuṇa, it appears, was the high god of the Indo-Irānian peoples before they broke up, for he has much in common with Ahura Mazda, the Zoroastrian god of light and righteousness, who also is conceived of as sitting in a glorious palace in heaven, surrounded by his ministers.

Of all the great gods of the *Ṛg-veda* the most popular was Indra, the god of war and rain. In one myth, the details of which are now lost but which is clearly alluded to in the *Ṛg-veda,* Indra appears as the creator of the cosmos. When the demons, led by the monstrous serpent Vṛtra, were attacking the gods and threatening their very existence, the young Indra, fortified by drinking three beakers of the sacred soma, went out alone to do battle with the demon. It was a tough fight and at times Indra was forced to turn and flee before his assailant; but in the end the monster was slain. From his dead body Indra fashioned the world.[6]

As a result of Indra's victory, the waters, which had been pent up in mountain caves by Vṛtra and his henchmen, were set free and flowed downward "for the welfare of man," overwhelming the dead body of the demon. This is generally taken as a rain-making myth, and Indra has always had the status of a rain god, bringing on the monsoon in June after destroying the evil forces that held it back.

In the *Ṛg-veda,* however, his chief function is that of a war leader. Not only did he defeat and slay the demons at the beginning of time, but also he still leads the Āryan hosts in their battles against the indigenous inhabitants. He is recorded as having destroyed, in years gone by, the stone fortresses of the Dāsas (one of the names by which the non-Āryans were known). He is a heavy drinker of the inebriating soma and appears to be likened to a young warlord of an Āryan tribe, fierce and dissolute but true to his word and loyal to his underlings. There is evidence that his star began to set before the compilation of the *Ṛg-veda* was completed, for a few hymns suggest that many men had lost faith in him.

Very important in the religion of the Āryans, though less strongly personified than Indra, was Agni, the fire god. The word *agni* is cognate with Latin *ignis* and means simply fire; thus in many passages it is not quite certain whether the reference is to normal earthly fire or the god Agni. It is through Agni that the sacrificial offerings are brought to the gods, and as an intermediary between gods and men he has a very important function. Every Āryan family has its domestic Agni in the family hearth fire, and thus Agni was very closely in touch with humans. Moreover, the nature of Agni gave rise to some of the earliest recorded Indian speculations about the relationship of the one and the many, a problem that has worried Indian thinkers from that day to this. In every family hearth there is Agni; Agni is hidden in the dark rain cloud and flashes forth as lightning; Agni blazes in the fire of the sacrifice. Agni is manifested in myriad ways throughout the world. Are there many Agnis or is there only one Agni, of which all the lesser Agnis are aspects? This question is not explicitly answered in the *Ṛg-veda,* but it seems that most of the singers favoured the second alternative. The typical Indian drive to reduce all apparently diversified phenomena to a single principle had already begun.

Soma, to whom all the hymns of the ninth book of the *Ṛgveda* are addressed, is the vague personification of a plant from which a potent beverage was made. Nowadays the few brāhmaṇic families who try to keep up the very ancient Vedic rituals make a rather bitter drink from a kind of wild rhubarb which they call soma, and the kindred Zoroastrians, called Pārsīs in India, make their *haoma* from a similar plant. The modern soma is quite innocuous, and it seems that at some time the original soma plant, which contained a powerful hallucinogen, was replaced by the ineffectual substitute that is used today. Soma was made as part of the sacrificial ritual, by pressing the plant between stones, mixing the juice with milk, and filtering it through a sheepskin. It cannot have been an alcoholic drink, since there was not enough time between manufacture and consumption to allow for the development of alcohol in large quantity. A suggestion made some years ago by the ethnomycologist R. Gordon Wasson is that soma was originally the agaric mushroom (*Amanita muscaria* [Fr. ex L.]), widespread in Central Asia and the Himālayan forests but not found in the hot, dry plains of India.[7] Later Soma was associated with the moon, but in the *Ṛgveda* he is simply the king of plants, bestower of immortality through the miraculous beverage he provides. The consumption of soma was permitted only during sacrifices, and it evidently produced vivid hallucinations, such as having a sense of growing to gigantic size and possessing superhuman strength or experiencing visions of the gods come down to join the worshippers on the sacrificial site. One hymn that describes a drunken Indra may also represent the feelings of a worshipper after having imbibed the sacred soma:

> Like wild winds
> the draughts have raised me up. Have I been drinking soma?

The draughts have borne me up,
as swift steeds a chariot. Have I been drinking soma?

Frenzy has come upon me,
as a cow to her dear calf. Have I been drinking soma?

As a carpenter bends the seat of a chariot
I bend this frenzy round my heart. Have I been drinking soma?

Not even as a mote in my eye
do the five tribes count with me. Have I been drinking soma?

The heavens above
do not equal one half of me. Have I been drinking soma?

In my glory I have passed beyond the sky
and the great earth. Have I been drinking soma?

I will pick up the earth,
and put it here or put it there. Have I been drinking soma?[8]

Several gods were connected with the sun. Sūrya, the sun god, means simply sun and, as with Agni, we are not always sure whether the Vedic poet is referring to the sun god or to the heavenly body after which he was named. Other solar gods were Savitṛ, the inspirer or emanator, Pūṣan, the invigorator or stimulator, and Viṣṇu, the permeator. The latter had a very important future ahead of him, but in the *Ṛg-veda* he is a comparatively minor god, loosely associated with the sun, who covers the three regions—earth, mid-space, and heaven—in three tremendous strides. The three strides of Viṣṇu were remembered in later times, and out of them a new legend developed concerning one of his *avatāras*, or incarnations.[9]

Another god who was to gain in importance in later times was Rudra. In the *Ṛg-veda* he is not a very popular god and has sinister aspects. He dwells in the mountains and rides the storm at the head of a host of storm spirits, the Maruts. In his role as the wild rider he may well have inherited features from a remote Indo-European past, for the storm god who rides across the sky is a feature of the myth and legend of many Indo-European peoples. Like the Greek Apollo, Rudra was an archer whose arrows brought disease; but also he knew the secrets of the healing herbs that grew on the mountaintops. Unlike most of the Āryan gods, he was feared rather than loved or admired, and unlike all the others, he was capricious. Even the righteous were not certain of escaping his attacks. Moral behaviour made no impression on him, and his arrows might be aimed at the righteous and sinners alike.

A class of shamans, or medicine men, the *munis,* were specially associated with Rudra. The word *muni* means silent and was used in later times to refer to ascetics of special sanctity; it was a term taken up especially by the Jains. The Vedic *munis* seem to have been wonder-workers who, after a long probation involving drinking poisonous substances, were accepted by the god and learnt his secrets. They knew the virtues of his herbs, and they had the power of flying through the air (that is, levitation). In one hymn (*Ṛg-veda* 10.136) they are referred to as "clothed in mind," which may simply imply that they were naked. The *munis* seem to have been outside the normal Āryan scheme of things, and it is possible that they were the survivors of some non-Āryan ascetic fraternity that was later loosely associated with the brāhmaṇic religion.

Besides the gods already mentioned, there were many others of secondary importance, to whom only a few hymns of the *Ṛg-veda* are addressed. Some of these seem to have been inherited from the remote Indo-European past; others were perhaps borrowed partially or wholly from the conquered people.

The hymns of the *Ṛg-veda* were chiefly composed for chanting at soma sacrifices where the sacred drink was pressed and drunk; animals were offered, and it was believed that the gods descended to the sacred grass (*barhis*) scattered over the sacrificial site and joined the worshippers in a sacrificial feast. Apparently it was thought that the gods made themselves visible to the worshippers, and gods and men mixed on almost equal terms.

Relations with the gods were generally friendly. Varuṇa inspired awe and Rudra fear, but the other gods were the good friends of the men who worshipped them and sacrificed to them, and they would unfailingly reward their devotees. In general the Āryans were on good terms with their gods.

The word *brāhmaṇ* (*brāhmaṇa*) in the sense of a priest occurs only once in the *Ṛg-veda,* in a very late hymn (10.90). The sacrificial priest (*ṛtvij*) was nevertheless a significant figure whose accurate performance of the ritual was essential for its success. Another priestly functionary was the *hotṛ,* whose duty it was to intone the appropriate hymns of the *Ṛg-veda* at the sacrifice. As with the sacrificing priest, he had to be very well trained, for an error in pronunciation or chant would render the entire sacrifice ineffectual. The most important of priestly functionaries, however, was the *purohita* ("he who is placed in the front"). It was the *purohita*'s duty to supervise the whole sacrifice. It seems that each tribal chief, or *rājan,* had at least one *purohita* who was responsible not only for conducting sacrifices but also for carrying out other rites for the welfare of the tribe. When the king went into battle, the *purohita* performed magical rituals to insure victory.

The universe for the Āryan was a simple one. At the top was heaven, the abode of the major gods, sun, moon, and stars. With them were the Fathers, the souls of the righteous dead who feasted forever in a realm comparable to the Nordic Valhalla. Heaven was divided from earth by a broad expanse of air, known as *antarikṣa,* where birds, clouds, and various types of demigods had their dwellings. Earth was flat; below it was a subterranean realm containing the spirits of the unrighteous dead which, in one passage, is referred to as the House of Clay. The Indians had not yet devised their complex cosmology, and there is no evidence that at this time they had any concept of the doctrine of transmigration, which later became characteristic of all Indian religion.

The religious life of the ordinary Āryan tribe member is scarcely hinted at in the *Ṛg-veda,* but the *Atharva-veda,* compiled at a comparatively late date, perhaps as late as 500 B.C.E., contains many spells of a religiomagical type and refers to deities not mentioned in the *Ṛg-veda.* If we can extrapolate from this text, we may assume that ordinary Āryans, as well as revering the great gods, had many lesser gods of a functional type who were helpful to them in their daily lives and who were worshipped in simple rituals and offerings that did not need the mediation of priests. Āryans were also very afraid of demons, who were believed to cause disease and other misfortunes.

The Āryans' rites of passage are referred to in certain late hymns of the *Ṛg-veda.* A lengthy wedding hymn shows that the Āryan ritual of marriage was a solemn religious ceremony involving the circumambulation of the sacred fire, which later was used to light the hearth fire of the newly married couple, and various other rituals intended to link husband and wife in an indissoluble bond and magically to insure their health and prosperity. Essentially it differed little from the contemporary Hindu marriage ceremony.

At least some of the dead were disposed of by cremation, as in present-day Hinduism, but there are suggestions of other types of funeral; it is possible that only the rich were cremated. Surprisingly there is no definite reference to the *śrāddha* ceremony, nowadays performed ten days after the funeral and optionally at intervals later. Since this rite has been looked on as essential for the welfare of the dead for some twenty-five hundred years or more, and since kindred rites are attested in other ancient Indo-European civilizations, we must assume that some such form of commemorative ritual took place.

The religion of the Āryans was oriented toward this world and the present life. The seers prayed to the gods that they might live for a hundred years, that they and their patrons might be rich and own thousands of cattle. But with the last book of the

Ṛg-veda, the tenth, a new phase of Indian religion begins, marked on the one hand by speculation, an imaginative search for a first principle, and on the other by the expansion of sacrificial ritual and the development of a sacrificial symbolism that was the main feature of the religious life reflected in later Vedic literature.

TWO

Early Speculations and the Later Sacrificial Cults

The Dawn of Philosophy in South Asia

Evidence of more speculative forms of thought comes at the end of a long tradition that saw humanity and the universe controlled by a host of divinities. These gods were not abandoned for philosophy but were revered in a cult that endeavoured to control cosmic forces by means of elaborate ritual sacrifices. In the last of the ten *maṇḍalas,* or books, of the *Ṛg-veda* we find a number of hymns whose contents are quite different from the main corpus of the collection and which in most cases seem to be later than the main collection. We gather this partly from their language and metre, which are somewhat closer to those of the standard classical Sanskrit, and partly from their content, which is much more speculative than that of previous hymns. These works introduce ideas, concepts, and entities that are not found in the earlier material of the *Ṛg-veda.* Where earlier the Āryan poets had been satisfied with alluding to well-known myths and legends, the poets were now showing a deep dissatisfaction with the older explanations and trying to find better ones. But they were not able to discuss the profound problems they were trying to solve in a rational manner, and so they expressed their new ideas by inventing new myths.

The main questions they asked themselves have been the bases of many religions and philosophical systems since the beginning of time and have not as yet been solved satisfactorily, either by philosophy or by science: Why is there a universe at all? Why is there not just nothingness?

To the keenest and most questioning minds of the times, the old legend of the great battle at the beginning of time between the god Indra and the demon Vṛtra must have seemed quite unsatisfactory as an explanation of the origin of all things. There is good evidence that many people were losing faith in Indra. Although many Āryans may have continued to believe the myth of the dragon slayer, there is evidence that others demanded more convincing explanations. Several alternative myths of creation or evolution were put forward to account for the existence of the world. Some of these formed bases on which much later thought was built; others made little impression and were soon almost forgotten.

The chronology of this process is extremely vague. Conventionally it is accepted that the main body of the *Ṛg-veda* was composed roughly between 1500 and 900 B.C.E. and that the recension of the text was made around the latter date; but the evidence is really very slight. All we can say with fair certainty is that all of the hymns must have been composed after roughly 1700 B.C.E., the latest possible date of the Harappā culture according to archaeological evidence. Between this date and the time of the Buddha (about 566–486 B.C.E. according to the most probable theory), a great body of oral Vedic literature was compiled, most of it obviously later than the *Ṛg-veda*. The data of archaeology give us little or nothing to help with the chronology of this literature, but one fact may have some relation to it.

The later Vedic texts show a much wider geographical horizon than does the *Ṛg-veda*. The focus of Ṛg-vedic culture is the Panjāb; in the later Vedic texts it is the Doāb, the region between the Yamunā and Gaṅgā (Ganges) rivers which became the heart of brāhmaṇic civilization. Much of the Ganges plain was then known and inhabited by Āryans. Numerous archaeological sites in the western Ganges area seem to contain levels dating back to this period, typified by well-made painted grey pottery and the beginnings of the use of iron. If any significant archaeological discoveries relevant to religion have been made, they are in Hastināpura, the capital of the Kuru tribe in the upper Ganges Doāb, where numerous cattle bones have been found which had certainly been cooked; some had been split to extract the marrow. This proves that at the time the Āryans did not hold cattle inviolable, as the later Hindus did, and that they were not vegetarians. The dating and spread of the Painted Grey Ware seem approximately to coincide with the period and area of later Vedic culture: the first half of the first millennium B.C.E., in the western part of the Ganges plain. This corresponds to the very time we believe that the Āryans were occupying the area and were creating the legends that led up to the great epic *Mahābhārata*.

Several hymns of the tenth book of the *Ṛg-veda* deal with the creation or evolution of the cosmos through entities or divinities newly devised to account for it. Among such entities we meet a Golden Embryo (Hiraṇyagarbha) out of whom the universe emanated, a god called All-Maker (Viśvakarman), a feminine entity called Voice or Sound (Vāc), and Time (Kāla). The first two divinities were consolidated into a new god called Prajāpati, the Lord of Progeny, conceived of as the father of the gods and of all things whatever.

Of these late speculative hymns, two are outstandingly important as evidence of the development of the thought of the time. One (*Ṛg-veda* 10.129) is particularly striking for its cosmic vision, its imaginative picture of a universe evolving out of a primal condition that was neither being nor nonbeing, neither cosmos nor chaos. The poet of this hymn shows, in fact, an incredible sophistication, when we remember that this hymn was composed, according to the accepted chronology, no later than 900 B.C.E., in an illiterate, mainly pastoral society.

Then even nothingness was not, nor existence.
  There was no air then, nor the heavens beyond it.
What covered it? Where was it? In whose keeping?
  Was there then cosmic water, in depths unfathomed?

Then there was neither death nor immortality,
  nor was there then the touch of night and day.
The One breathed windlessly and self-sustaining.
  There was that One then, and there was no other.

At first there was only darkness wrapped in darkness.
  All this was only unilluminated water.
That One which came to be, enclosed in nothing,
  arose at last, born of the power of heat.

In the beginning desire descended on it—
  that was the primal seed, born of the mind.
The sages who have searched their hearts with wisdom
  know that which is is kin to that which is not.

And they have stretched their cord across the void,
  and know what was above, and what below.
Seminal powers made fertile mighty forces.
  Below was strength, and over it was impulse.

But, after all, who knows, and who can say
  whence it all came, and how creation happened?
The gods themselves are later than creation,
  so who knows truly whence it has arisen?

Whence all creation had its origin,
  he, whether he fashioned it or whether he did not,
he who surveys it all from highest heaven,
  he knows—or maybe even he does not know.[1]

This hymn is the starting point of many themes of Indian philosophy. *Sat* and *asat*, being and nonbeing, real and unreal, truth and lie, are common principles in later Vedic thought. It seems that they were used in many early Vedic contexts to imply respectively the cosmos—the abode of gods, humanity, and animals—and the chaos—the haunt of demons and terrible monsters. Out of the primal stuff emerged a desire or urge; the term used here, *kāma*, has sexual overtones, as has the English word *desire,* but there is no necessity for such implications in this context. The effect of desire was to produce *tapas,* the supernatural "heat" that was believed to develop out of asceticism. Thus the universe evolved. But after all, who can tell exactly what happened at the beginning of all things? Even the gods were not there then, and they do not know the truth. Possibly the high god Prajāpati knows, but even this is uncertain—"or maybe even he does not know."

This hymn is possibly the oldest expression of philosophic doubt in the literature of the world, and it forms a landmark in the history of Indian thought. It is the work of a questing spirit striving to express in language concepts never before expressed, who would not accept ready-made myths in the search for the secret of existence, who was willing to admit ignorance rather than put forward another unprovable theory. Here are the beginnings of the great schools of Indian philosophy, which strove to reduce all spiritual, mental, and physical processes to a complex system in order to point the way to release from the round of birth and death.

Equally important, if less beautiful from the literary point of view, is the well-known *Puruṣasūkta,* "Hymn of the (Primeval) Man" (*Ṛg-veda* 10.90). This, from its style, appears to be one of the most recently composed hymns of the collection, probably later in composition than 1000 B.C.E. It tells of a mighty giant, larger even than the universe as we know it, who was at first the only being in existence. This primal being, feeling lonely, decided to divide itself and produced Virāj (Shining Forth), a feminine entity. A later verse, found in the *Bṛhadāraṇyaka Upaniṣad* (1.4), informs us that the mating of Puruṣa and Virāj produced a second Puruṣa, and after him the gods. At this time, even before the universe existed, the gods decided to sacrifice to their father, the first Puruṣa. As the victim they chose his eldest son, the second Puruṣa.[2] He was slain and dismembered, and from the parts of his body the universe, including its human inhabitants, was fashioned.

When they divided the Man,
into how many parts did they divide him?
What was his mouth, what was his arms,
what were his thighs and his feet?

The brāhmaṇ was his mouth,
of his arms was made the warrior,
his thighs became the vaiśya [peasant]
of his feet the śūdra [serf] was born.

The moon arose from his mind,
from his eye was born the sun,
from his mouth Indra and Agni,
from his breath the wind was born.

From his navel came the air,
from his head there came the sky,
from his feet the earth, the four quarters from his ear,
thus they fashioned the worlds.

With Sacrifice the gods sacrificed to Sacrifice—
these were the first of the sacred laws.
These mighty beings reached the sky,
where are the eternal spirits, the gods.[3]

The new myth of the Puruṣa, the primal man or person, marks another stage in the development of Hindu thought. Parallel with the growth in cosmic speculation and with new concepts of the evolution of the universe by a natural process, as reflected in the Hymn of Creation, emerged another tendency, placing great emphasis on sacrifice. The *Puruṣasūkta* represents the triumph of a sort of sacrificial mysticism. The universe was created not out of the body of a primeval monster slain in battle, not, as in the Hymn of the Golden Embryo, by the bursting of a primeval egg floating in the ocean of chaos, not by a mighty process, almost indescribable in words, as in the Hymn of Creation, but by a sacrifice. The conclusions drawn from these premises are significant.

Among the entities produced from the gigantic victim were the four estates of the Hindu social order. This is the first appearance of the four, brought together in a single system. Since the four classes are numbered with cattle, horses, and sheep as products of the body of the giant, it is clear that they are already thought of as separate, and no amount of special pleading by a few scholars can controvert the obvious fact that they are ranged in hierarchical order. From the head of the Puruṣa came the brāhmaṇ, the intermediary between gods and humans, and thanks to his knowledge of sacrificial ritual, he keeps the world going. From the arms came the *rājanya,* later called *kṣatriya,* the warrior and ruler; the trunk of the victim yielded the *vaiśya,* the peasant and craftsman; while from the feet, the humblest and lowest of the limbs, was made the *śūdra,* the non-Āryan serf who had gradually drawn closer to his masters and more and more accepted their mythology and ritual, until he achieved a position, albeit a very subordinate one, in the Āryan social order.

There is evidence to show that when the Āryans first came to India—at least five hundred years before the composition of the *Puruṣasūkta*—there was a class distinction between patricians and plebeians within the Vedic tribes. A special class of priest, forgotten by the time of this hymn, may also have existed in those days. But the original Āryan class system seems to have been much looser than the four *varṇas,* or classes, of the brāhmaṇic scheme. Originally there were occasional promotions from a lower to a higher class, and intermarriage seems to have been permitted, as indeed it had been in India for centuries. From then on, however, even down to the present day, the four rigid classes formed the norm of Āryan and Hindu society. That norm has not always been followed in fact, but in theory it is eternal and inviolable.

Thus, nearly three thousand years ago, the Āryans tried to establish a fairly strictly partitioned social system. With the sanction of their religion they largely succeeded in doing this, and the four *varṇas* became the social norm. The word *varṇa* also means colour, and the pigmentation of the skin may have had a hand in the evolution of the system. In the *Ṛg-veda* there is reference to "the colour of the Āryans" and "the colour of the Dāsas," the latter being a term for the indigenous inhabitants of northwestern India, a term that soon came to mean slave or serf. We are not told explicitly what the colours were, but it is assumed that the phrases refer to fair and dark skins respectively. Probably the Āryans, when they first entered India, though they were far from being Nordic blondes, had skins and hair little if at all darker than those of the modern European, especially in the Mediterranean areas; the indigenous inhabitants, on the other hand, were probably various shades of brown. The *varṇa* system may reflect an attempt to prevent further miscegenation, which was looked on as very objectionable. Though nowadays many Indians, influenced by egalitarian ideas, are strongly opposed to segregation, the sense of colour is still very strong in India.

Sacrifical Ritual of the Later Vedas

The *Ṛg-veda* is only the first constituent of a great body of literature known as Vedic by Western scholars and classed by Hindu tradition as *śruti,* "that which has been (directly) heard," as distinct from later religious literature, such as the epics, the Purāṇas, and the *Dharma Śāstras,* which is known as *smṛti,* "that which has been remembered." The latter class is considered less sacred than the former.

Of the four Vedas—the *Ṛg-*, *Yajur-*, *Sāma-*, and *Atharva-vedas*—the *Sāma-veda* is a recension of certain hymns and verses mostly borrowed from the *Ṛg-veda,* arranged for singing in a somewhat more elaborate manner than the simple chanting of the *Ṛg-veda.* Less than a hundred stanzas of the *Sāma-veda* are original, and this text is of interest only to specialists. The *Yajur-veda* is a series of prose formulas (later known as *mantras*) for utterance in the course of the sacrifice. The text is found in five main recensions, of which four are known as the Black *Yajur-veda* and one as the White. The distinction between the two types of recension (*saṃhitā*)[4] is that the Black contain, as well as the formulas themselves, brief explanations of their significance and their place in the ritual, while the White contains nothing but the formulas, with the explanations, instructions, and interpretations being reserved for an appendix, or commentary (Brāhmaṇa).

The fourth Veda, the *Atharva-veda,* is different in character from the other three, which, though they may contain a certain amount of other material, all relate to the sacrificial rituals. The *Atharva-veda* has little or no relationship to the sacrifice. It is in fact chiefly a collection of spells, charms, imprecations, and incantations, most of them of appreciable literary value but of very little profound religious significance. They belong to a stratum in which religion overlaps with magic. Here we may find spells for casting out demons that cause disease, formulas to restore the affection of a mistress whose love has grown cold, charms to insure success in battle and in trade. Since in most of these poems one or more of the great gods is invoked, they must be considered religious texts, but religious on a rather low and practical level. Besides these magicoreligious poems, the *Atharva-veda* also contains a considerable number of lengthy speculative and mystical hymns, similar to some of those in the tenth book of the *Ṛg-veda.* Some of these hymns seem to continue the speculations of that book, while others branch out on new tracks. Among these are the hymns to an entity referred to as Skambha, the Pillar or Support of the Universe; to Prāṇa, the Breath of Life; to Kāma, Desire, personified as the primeval being; to Kāla, Time; and to similar personified principles, many of which, in fact, played no important part in later thought.

The brāhmaṇs who composed the hymns of the *Atharva-veda* were not sacrificial priests, and their poems, accumulated and orally edited, were not readily accepted as canonical. This is shown by the fact that in many early texts only three Vedas are referred to in place of the orthodox four of later times, with no reference to the *Atharva-veda*.

As the sacrificial ritual became more complex, further texts were composed to explain its mysteries and symbolism. All, as far as we can tell, were orally composed and transmitted. These texts were called *Brāhmaṇas*. The word is the same as that used for the brāhmaṇ priest but is neuter in gender. The word *brahman*[5] originally meant magical force, especially the supernatural power inherent in certain utterances. Later, as speculation about *brahman* developed, the word was applied to the ultimate impersonal being that underlay the whole universe. In these senses it is a neuter noun, and it is capitalized to distinguish the two meanings. Later still, the same word in the masculine, usually transcribed with a long final vowel (*Brahmā*) came to mean one of the greatest of the gods, in some places and periods looked on as the high god, who developed out of the previously mentioned Prajāpati. *Brāhmaṇa,* a secondary noun, derived from *brahman,* came to mean a priest only at the end of the Ṛg-vedic period. In most modern languages of northern India the final *-a* is not sounded, and so it is commonly written *brāhmaṇ* or *brăhmin,* the latter being a solecism or corruption, without justification. These different but cognate words should not be confused. The following spellings are regularly used in this book:

Brahman	*Supernatural power, the absolute world spirit.*
Brahmā	*The god.*
brāhmaṇ	*A member of the priestly order (also brāhmaṇa).*
Brāhmaṇa	*A Vedic text of the brāhmaṇic class.*

The Brāhmaṇas, each theoretically appended to one of the Vedas, are lengthy prose texts, mostly concerned with the sacrifice and its symbolism. Their composition probably began around 900 B.C.E. and continued for several centuries. They are not among the most inspiring of India's religious literature, and it is not surprising that in the past they have been rather neglected by specialists. Nevertheless they contain much that is of interest and value, and they provide considerable evidence of the progress of thought from the *Ṛg-veda* to the period of the Upaniṣads, when mystical gnosis became a very important factor in the religious life of India.

There are several Brāhmaṇas. Of these, the most important are the *Aitareya Brāhmaṇa* and the *Śatapatha Brāhmaṇa,* the *Brāhmaṇa* of 100 Paths. The latter, a very lengthy text, is the crowning product of the thought of the period, bringing together much that is to be found in the earlier Brāhmaṇas. It is attributed to the sage Yājñavalkya, who seems to have been a historical personage and one of considerable importance in the history of Hinduism. The *Śatapatha* is probably the latest of the important Brāhmaṇa texts, the last of a long series. It may have been composed in the seventh century B.C.E., but its date is very uncertain.

The ideology behind the Brāhmaṇa literature looks back to the *Puruṣasūkta* of the *Ṛg-veda,* describing the great sacrifice of the primal man at the beginning of time. From this it is clear that the universe emerged from sacrifice, and therefore sacrifice is fundamental to the universal process. The world began with a stupendous sacrifice performed by the gods. To maintain it in good working order constant repetitions of that original sacrifice are necessary. Otherwise the universe would quickly degenerate and chaos would come again. Indeed the gods themselves are dependent on sacrifice. This means that the only persons qualified to carry out large-scale sacrifices, the brāhmaṇs, are in a sense greater than the gods. At this time the brāhmaṇs made very exaggerated claims and pretended to a status higher than that of kings, which perhaps in some contexts they were granted. It is certain, however, that they were not always accorded the respect that they claimed, though at all times orthodox kings treated them with great deference. The claims of the brāhmaṇs were strengthened by the belief that the sacrifice had to be performed with scrupulous accuracy; otherwise it would prove ineffectual and would do more harm than good. Thus, by deliberately making minor errors in the ritual, the brāhmaṇ could, putatively, ruin the patron who sponsored the sacrifice and even cause harm to the cosmos itself. Hence, for those who accepted the brāhmaṇ's doctrine of sacrifice, the brāhmaṇ was at the same time the supreme social servant and the most dangerous of potential enemies.

The daily domestic sacrifices, in theory performed by every Āryan, are not discussed at length in the Brāhmaṇas but are treated in somewhat later texts, the *Gṛhya Sūtras,*[6] which lay down the norms of the life of the Āryan of good caste. These rituals, with roots in the remote Indo-European past, are still performed by some orthodox brāhmaṇic families, although among most Hindus their place has been taken by *pūjā,* the worship of the gods in the form of images. These sacrifices centred on the domestic fire, where Agni, the fire god, received the offerings and conveyed them to the other gods. They were performed especially at dawn and dusk and involved the recitation of the proper Vedic *mantras* while pouring offerings of milk and ghee (clarified butter) on the fire, followed by libations of water.

More complicated sacrifices were the *darśapūrṇamāsas* at the beginning of the two lunar fortnights of the months according to the Hindu calendar, the days of the new and full moons. Though this sacrifice was regulated by the moon, it was not directed to Soma, who by this time had become the moon god, but to several of the great gods of the Vedic pantheon. Yet more elaborate was the *caturmāsya,* performed at four-monthly intervals at the beginning of each of the three seasons of the Vedic calendar. These sacrifices were comparatively inexpensive and did not normally involve the sacrifice of animals or the pressing of soma, which by now had probably become quite innocuous. This was not the case with the *agniṣṭoma,* an annual ceremony originally taking place in spring but often performed in other parts of the year. The *agniṣṭoma* could be compressed into one day, but it might last much longer and be developed into a very complicated and expensive ritual, involving the pressing of soma and the slaughter of animal victims.

These rituals were comparatively simple and could be performed by ordinary tribesmen of the three higher classes who had undergone the proper rite of initiation. In this period, however, certain new ceremonies of a very lengthy and complicated type appeared, especially devised, it seems, for kings and wealthy tribal chiefs.[7] They involved the slaughter of numerous animals and consisted of a whole series of rites, sometimes lasting over a year. Three of these great royal sacrifices were particularly outstanding, and their importance is much greater than it at first appears to be, for, though they have long lapsed into desuetude, their effects on political attitudes have been felt all through the history of India, and the ideas behind them survive in some measure even to the present day, especially among a few brāhmaṇic groups in southern India.

The *rājasūya* sacrifice was a royal consecration ceremony, and it was thought in orthodox circles that a king who had not performed this series of rituals and sacrifices was not a true *rājan.* After a long series of preliminary sacrifices, lasting perhaps for as long as a year, the king was anointed with a mixture of liquids, including water, ghee, and honey, first by the brāhmaṇs and then by representatives of the other classes among his subjects. The rituals raised him to virtually divine status, at least for the duration of the sacrifice, and he emerged from it strengthened in his power, with a divine charisma upon him.

The king who had undergone this royal consecration might, after reigning for some years, further strengthen his kingly power by ordering the performance of the *vājapeya* (drink of vitality) sacrifice. This too was a complex and expensive process, the kernel of which was a series of rituals designed to prove the king's continued strength and vitality—for instance a chariot race and a game of *akṣas,*[8] which the king invariably won. In fact the *vājapeya* was essentially a rejuvenation ceremony.

Most important of the great royal ceremonies was the *aśvamedha,* the horse sacrifice. It was the ambition of every king of importance to perform at least one *aśvamedha* in the course of his reign, for thus he would not only insure a heaven for himself and prosperity for his land and people but also establish his own importance and prove his power and influence over all other kings in the vicinity of his kingdom.

The *aśvamedha* involved a programme of activities lasting for well over a year. In the early spring a specially chosen stallion was consecrated and released to wander at will. With him travelled one hundred other horses and a band of four hundred chosen young warriors, whose duty it was to follow the horse wherever he led them. If he wandered beyond the bounds of the realm of the king who released him, the local rulers were summoned to render homage and tribute. If they refused to do so, the warriors following the horse gave battle. The failure of an *aśvamedha* is not unknown in tradition, but it rarely occurred, for no king in his right senses would carry out such an expensive ceremony without fair certainty that it would succeed. At the end of the year the horse was returned to the capital of the king and sacrificed by strangulation or suffocation, together with a large number of other animals.

A feature of the *aśvamedha* which has aroused considerable comment is the sexual character of one of the concluding ceremonies. The chief queen lay down beside the body of the sacrificed horse and simulated copulation with him, to the accompaniment of obscene remarks by the priests and nobles standing by. This shows that the *aśvamedha* had some of its roots in very ancient fertility ceremonies, and its purpose was partly to ensure the productivity of the land, represented by the queen. Nevertheless the main emphasis of the *aśvamedha* was on political power. The political system envisaged by those who developed this sacrifice was what has elsewhere been called quasi-feudal, wherein a powerful overlord received homage and tribute from a circle of less powerful subordinates. If in the course of the horse's wanderings any king had tried to block his passage and had been defeated in the ensuing battle, there was no question of such a king being dethroned or of the annexation of his lands by the conqueror. The defeated king was merely expected to appear at the final ceremony and to accept the overlordship of the victor. Thus the tradition of the *aśvamedha* did not encourage the building of solid centralized empires; rather, it visualized a loose federation of kingdoms under a single overlord, all virtually independent in respect of their internal affairs.

These great royal ceremonies were performed by early kings, but later a secular countertradition of centralized authority gained ground, and for a few centuries there are no records of the performance of the *aśvamedha*. In the second century B.C.E., however, it was revived, and occasional records of it appear down to the tenth century. The *rājasūya* was replaced by a simpler anointing ceremony (*rājābhiṣeka*), which did not involve the slaughter of animals, and it eventually lost more and more favour among the brāhmaṇ mentors of the kings.

The age of the great sacrifices passed, but they were remembered in tradition, and they left their mark on later Hinduism. Recently a few such sacrifices have been performed by a certain group of brāhmaṇs in Mahārāshtra and Keralā. These fairly faithfully reproduced the archaic rituals but did not involve the slaughter of animals. The spirit behind these sacrifices is largely dead in modern Hinduism.

The great royal sacrifices were not, however, mere artificial inventions of the brāhmaṇs designed to boost the power of the king and, indirectly, of themselves. The *aśvamedha,* for instance, involved a series of secondary activities in which all the populace might take at least a passive part. These included, among other things, the recitation of stirring ballads describing the exploits of the king's ancestors, as well as dance and song. One may imagine the feelings of the ordinary subject as he stood with his family at a respectful distance watching the slaughter of literally hundreds of animals tied to posts, in their forefront the sacrificial horse. It was a tremendously solemn event. Nowhere is it stated what became of the bodies of all these animals. Some parts of them were incinerated as offerings to the gods, as among the Hebrews and Greeks. Much of the meat of the victims must have been eaten, as is the case with the goat sacrifice of modern Hinduism. Probably nearly all of the populace had some share in the sacrificial offerings, and the meat of the animals killed was not wholly wasted. These sacrifices were in fact occasions for rejoicing, not only for kings and their courtiers, but for the whole populace.

THREE

The Development of Philosophy and the Origin of the Doctrine of Transmigration

The German philosopher Karl Jaspers posited in *The Origin and Goal of History*[1] that, between the eighth and the fourth centuries B.C.E., great changes took place in the religious life of people in all the civilized parts of the world. Some of the wisest individuals of the times began thinking independently and individually. Dissatisfied with the traditional mythologies as explanations of the cosmos and humanity's place in it, they put forward new doctrines, more rational and simpler than those that went before, with a much deeper ethical content. Among these sages were the Greek philosophers, the Hebrew prophets, Zarathuštra in what is now Irān, and Confucius, Lao-tsu,[2] and others in China. Last but not least, there arose in India a series of hermits and sages who produced the mystical thought contained in the series of texts called Upaniṣads, and also a number of wandering ascetics who repudiated the brāhmaṇic system root and branch and put forward thoroughly heterodox doctrines.

Jaspers asserts that after these great thinkers the world was never the same again. Traditional religion was slowly modified by the new ideas to produce the great religious and philosophical systems that prevail today. Moreover, there is no good explanation of why these developments took place when they did throughout the world, taking different forms in lands far apart, between which there was little or no contact. Jaspers called this time the axial period (*Achzenzeit*).[3] In India, in any case, there were so many changes and developments in religion during this time that it marked a real turning point in the spiritual and intellectual life of the land; it saw the virtual beginning of such typical aspects of Indian religion as the doctrines of transmigration and nonviolence, organized asceticism, mystical gnosis in search of release (*mokṣa*) from the cycle of birth and death, and many lesser features of Hinduism, not to speak of the rise of heterodoxies such as Buddhism and Jainism.

This is not to say that premonitions of the axial period may not be traced in earlier Vedic literature. Speculation about probable first causes is as old as the later hymns of the *Ṛg-veda,* and traces of mysticism and asceticism are also found there. These tendencies were present long before they produced their first fruits in the beautiful series of texts called the Upaniṣads.

The word *upaniṣad* means literally sitting near, from which derives the sense of secret session. The Upaniṣads fall into two main categories. The earlier ones are in prose and take the form of anthologies of the teachings of various sages. Some of these teachers are in fact gods, others are legendary seers (*ṛṣis*) of the remote past, but many appear to be historical figures. The earlier prose Upaniṣads gave way to later ones in verse or mixed verse and prose, more unitary in structure, the composition of which continued into the Middle Ages. There is a canonical list of 108 Upaniṣads,[4] but of these only thirteen are considered authentic in the sense that they were compiled early as genuine appendices to the Vedas and Brāhmaṇas.

There is also a category of texts known as Āraṇyakas, Forest Texts, midway in style between the Brāhmaṇas and Upaniṣads. One of the oldest Upaniṣads, the *Bṛhadāraṇyaka,* the Highest

Āraṇyaka, shows clearly in its title how the one class of text evolved out of the other. But the Āraṇyakas contain little of the exalted mysticism of the Upaniṣads, being mainly concerned with the same theme as the Brāhmaṇas, the cosmic symbolism of the sacrificial ritual. They are of importance and interest principally to specialists.

Dating the Upaniṣads with accuracy is impossible. It is evident that they are later than the Vedas and most of the Brāhmaṇas. If the recension of the *Ṛg-veda* took place around 1000 or 900 B.C.E., as most scholars believe, the earliest Upaniṣads could hardly be earlier than 700–600 B.C.E. Many Indian scholars and others, however, would date them much earlier. The latest of the thirteen principal Upaniṣads, the *Maitrī Upaniṣad,* was certainly composed at a time when Buddhism was well known and fairly widespread, no earlier than 300 B.C.E., and perhaps considerably later.

Great changes had taken place in India since the days of the *Ṛg-veda.* The Āryans had expanded eastward as far as the borders of the modern state of Bihār, and in the south they knew the Narmadā River. Most of them had ceased to be nomadic and were settled in permanent villages, where they cultivated the soil as well as bred cattle. Iron was steadily replacing bronze as their main metal. A few small cities had arisen, centring on fortified palaces where local kings resided with their henchmen, and there was a much greater range of trades and professions than in the earlier period. The system of the four classes (*varṇas*) had hardened, with the brāhmaṇ claiming ritual superiority and often getting it, and the *rājanya,* increasingly called by his more usual later appellation, *kṣatriya,* enforcing his own political and social superiority. We have seen how the newly elaborated sacrifices of the Brāhmaṇas might have been devised to strengthen the power and prestige of kings as well as of the priests who served them.

The third class, the *vaiśya,* appears at this early time to have consisted chiefly of free peasants, but it also included a growing range of merchants, professional men, and skilled craftsmen. These three classes, brāhmaṇ, *kṣatriya,* and *vaiśya,* became known as twice-born (*dvija*), from the fact that their boys underwent an initiation ceremony called *upanayana,* which allowed them to hear, study, and recite the Vedas, forbidden to *śūdras* and women. Initiated members of the twice-born classes were distinguished by the sacred cord (*yajñopavīta,* or, in Hindī, *janeo*), which they wore over their left shoulder and under their right arm and never removed.[5]

The *śūdras,* the lowest of the four classes, were originally serfs and labourers, with few religious or legal rights, whose main duty was to wait on the members of the three twice-born classes. The status of many *śūdra* castes, however, steadily improved. Some became independent peasants and craftsmen, and a few even gained political power and became kings.

There is every reason to believe that this was a period of great material progress. Yet this economic and material expansion is not well reflected in the literature. Parallel with the increasing complexity of the sacrifice there was a development of pessimism about the validity and permanence of life in heaven, along with a growth of ascetic practices. Whether any practical or social factors encouraged this growth of pessimism is not completely clear, but the economic progress must have been accompanied by considerable social change. The Āryans of the *Ṛgveda* were organized tribally. The sense of belonging to a tribe must have given psychological security and a sense of kinship to people. In this period, tribal bonds were loosened. Chiefs of tribes became kings of a certain territory, and their subjects found themselves increasingly merged in a melting pot of people which included not only Āryans from many tribes, but also non-Āryans among the lower social orders, and even some non-Āryans who had raised themselves to important positions in the land. It is only at a somewhat later period that we get clear evidence of belief in a decline of society from a happy golden age to a present one fraught with evil and likely to get worse, but there is good reason to believe that such ideas began around this time.

Pessimism showed itself in various ways among the authors of Brāhmaṇas and the Vedic literature, but chiefly in the ideas about the afterlife. Belief in the World of the Fathers, the cheerful Āryan Valhalla, continued, but doubts arose as to whether life in the other world was eternal. It was explicitly stated that heavenly joys were also transient and that "from world to world deaths find one out." The righteous individual who cares for personal spiritual welfare thus had to prepare not only for an earthly death but for an indeterminate number of later deaths. There is no clear evidence that this involved belief in the transmigration of the soul, such as appeared in later times, but it was certainly a step in that direction. The best the Brāhmaṇa literature could offer as a means of triumphing over death in the other world was mystical knowledge of the fact that Death was, in fact, one; though there were many individual deaths, they were all really one great divinity, and by propitiating him with the magic word *svāhā* (hail) one would escape his clutches in the afterlife.[6] Probably few found this solution very convincing.

Another sign of the times was the growth of asceticism. Certain men had long been given to ascetic practices. They probably began as shamanistic ordeals performed to achieve magical powers, such as we see in the case of the *munis* of the *Ṛg-veda*. Temporary fasting and celibacy were laid down as preliminaries to the greater sacrifices. At this time, around the beginning of the later Vedic period, there arose the belief that by asceticism a man accumulated *tapas*. The original meaning of this word is heat, but it came increasingly to mean a supernormal power that developed in a man as a result of such practices as fasting, maintaining difficult and painful postures for long periods, and other forms of self-mortification. By the time of the Buddha (about 500 B.C.E.), if we are to believe the Pāli scriptures of the Buddhists, the most spectacular and what we might call psychopathic forms of self-torture—such as sitting or lying on beds of thorns, hanging upside down from branches of trees, and keeping a limb in the same position for months until it atrophied—were already being practised by certain ascetics. The motives for asceticism were no doubt manifold. The desire for supernormal power was always a significant factor, but there was also a sense of guilt, the desire to expunge the effects of sin or ritual shortcoming, and a further, increasingly important motive was the desire for security in the other world.

Some men became so devoted to ascetic practices that they gave up their homes and lived as hermits in huts or caves in the forests. The ascetic discipline varied in its intensity. Some men took their wives with them and raised families in hermit colonies. Others were completely alone, subjecting themselves to long fasts and other forms of self-discipline in the depths of the jungles. Still others did not remain in the forests but wandered about from village to village, begging their food and arguing with opponents.

These men who opted out of society may in many cases have had psychological motives: loss of faith in the old verities, dissatisfaction with the way the world was going, ennui, weltschmerz, *noia,* fear of the future. But there was also a positive side to asceticism. There is enough to show that many men embraced an ascetic order and left their homes, abandoning society with a great sense of relief, in the hope not only of finding peace of mind but also of plunging in and discovering the ultimate meaning of existence and the supreme secrets of the cosmos.

It was among these people, it seems, that the doctrines of *saṃsāra* and *karman,* closely linked in the system of transmigration, developed. Almost everybody in the Western world knows something about the basic principle of transmigration, that the soul passes from body to body according to its works. Most forms of life are linked in this cycle of birth and death and rebirth: gods, demigods, human beings, animals down to the humblest worms, demons, souls in torment in the nether regions.[7] This constant passage of the soul from one body to another is known as *saṃsāra,* a term commonly used to imply "the world," in its everyday material sense.

The nature of the new life to which the soul passes is determined by *karman,* literally action, work, deed. As a man acts in one life, so he enjoys happiness or sorrow in the next. In popular Hinduism the punishment is made to fit the crime. The man who was born with a deformed arm, for instance, must be expiating an act of violence done by that arm in his previous life. The luck of the rich and successful is the result of former benevolence. Insatiable gluttons may be reborn as pigs; men of violence may become tigers and leopards.[8] There are terrible purgatories below the earth, where the souls of great sinners suffer for many millenniums, until they expunge the worst of their sins and are given another chance on earth. On the other hand the virtuous enjoyed immense periods of bliss in one of the heavens before returning to earth for a new life that might lead even higher.

These are the beliefs of nearly all Indians, other than Muslims, Christians, and Pārsīs, down to the present day. They appear to have been almost universally held in the Ganges plain as early as the Buddha's time, because in the Buddhist scriptures we find a discussion of whether transmigration exists or not. It was, therefore, taken for granted. Yet there are no clear references to transmigration in the Vedic literature before the Upaniṣads. People of the Vedic period did not generally believe in the passage of the soul from one body to another. From these texts it appears that the doctrine began as a new and strange one. The idea that it was held widely by the non-Āryan peoples of the Ganges plain has no basis in any source—it is little more than surmise, based on the fact that some primitive peoples in various parts of the world believed in a form of transmigration, often connected with totemism: The soul of a member of a given tribe was reborn as an animal of the species that his tribe held as the totem, and vice versa. But there is no evidence of such a belief among the tribal peoples of the Indian hills, either in those times or nowadays.[9]

In fact all the evidence goes to show that the doctrine of transmigration began as a secret one, held by only a few sages. One passage in the *Śatapatha Brāhmaṇa* seems to indicate that Indians began fearing the possibility of death in heaven. It does not suggest that souls returned to earth when their merit was exhausted, as is the belief of later Indian religions. The first clear references to transmigration occur in the *Bṛhadāraṇyaka Upaniṣad,* perhaps the oldest and certainly the longest of the Upaniṣads, and was associated with the great sage Yājñavalkya. Yājñavalkya came to the court of King Janaka of Videha (now northern Bihār), who organized a great discussion among the wise men of the land. Yājñavalkya carried the day and received immense prizes in the form of cattle. Later, we are told, he became an ascetic, and his touching farewell to his favourite wife Maitreyī is one of the most famous passages in the Upaniṣadic literature.[10]

Here at Janaka's court (*Bṛhadāraṇyaka Upaniṣad* 3.2), Yājñavalkya is questioned by another sage, Jāratkārava Ārtabhāga. He answers all Jāratkārava's questions until the last one.

> Yājñavalkya, when a man dies, his voice enters fire, his breath enters the wind, his eyes the sun, his mind the moon, his ears the quarters, his body the earth, his self (*ātman*) space, the hair of his body the plants, the hair of his head the trees, and his blood and semen repose in the waters. Where is that man then?

But Yājñavalkya was unwilling to answer in public. "Ārtabhāga," he said, "take my hand. We two alone must know about this. It is not for us to make public." Then we are told, "Together they went off and talked with each other." What they discussed was *karman,* what they praised was *karman.* "By good works a man becomes good (*puṇya*), by evil works evil (*pāpa*)."[11] Then Jāratkārava was silent.

If we are to take this passage at face value the doctrine of *karman* was invented by Yājñavalkya, for when he said, "We two alone must know about this," he was, at the time, the *only* person who knew the secret. We note that the compiler has carefully avoided giving Yājñavalkya's words. He has literary skills and thinks logically, and if he had purported to give Yājñavalkya's exact words, as he does elsewhere, it would be evident that either a third party had listened to the conversation or Jāratkārava had betrayed the secret. This passage, as a portrayal of the author or compiler of the doctrine, represents the very beginning of the doctrine of *karman*.

Elsewhere Yājñavalkya elaborates on this doctrine and proposes it explicity. This seems to have taken place during a later visit to King Janaka (*Bṛhadāraṇyaka Upaniṣad* 4.3.1). Elsewhere in the work (4.4), we are told that the self or soul is like a looping caterpillar, which draws itself up at the tip of a blade of grass in order to pass to another, or like the gold used by a goldsmith who forges a new and more beautiful object from an old and broken one. Now Yājñavalkya tells Janaka in public the new doctrine that he had earlier told Jāratkārava in secret: As humans act, so they become. Whoever does good becomes good, whoever does evil becomes evil (4.4.5). Yājñavalkya then elaborates further:

> Some have said, "The person consists only of desire"; [thus it is said,] "As is his desire, so is his will; as is his will, so will he act; as he acts, so will he attain."
>
> To whatever his mind and character is attached, to that a man goes with his works. He reaps the reward of the deeds he does on earth and comes back again to the world of action. [But,] he who is free from desire . . . , being Brahman itself, goes to Brahman. . . .
>
> When all desires in the heart are released, then the mortal becomes immortal and he attains Brahman. (4.4.5–7)

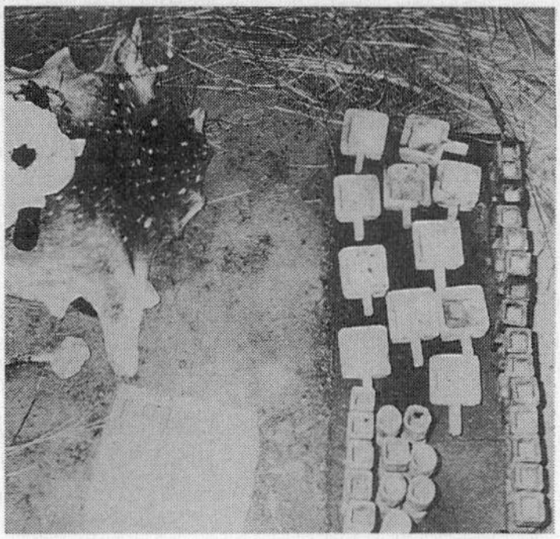

1–7. SCENES FROM A MODERN CELEBRATION OF THE VEDIC VĀJAPEYA RITUAL. (*South India, twentieth century; collector: James A. Santucci.*) The one-day Vājapeya or "Drink of Vitality" usually took place in autumn. Commissioned only by a Brāhmaṇ or a Kṣatriya, it was intended to secure the sacrificer's success and prosperity. The ancient festival involved a chariot race in which the sacrificer was victor, the sacrifice of animals and the offering and consumption of soma and wine, and required the participation of the sacrificer's wife. The scenes show in sequence: (1) display of ritual implements (the black antelope skin representing the sacrificed animal); (2) the purchase of stalks of the (surrogate) soma plant to be pressed into the intoxicating drink; (3) the churning to kindle the sacrificial fire, into which the oblations are made and carried to the gods by fire god (Agni); (*cont.*)

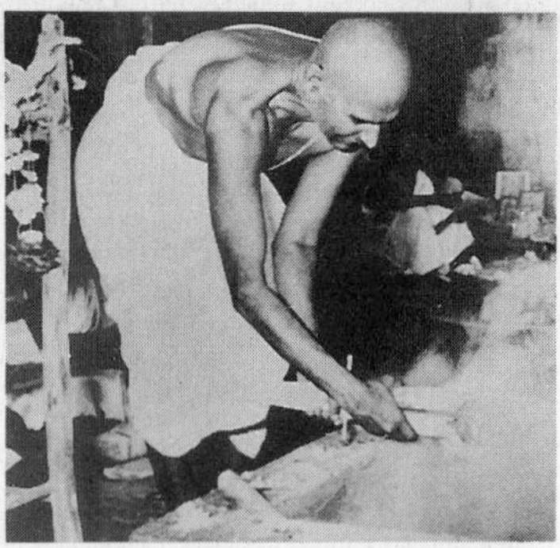

(4–6) various offerings, including soma and wine, in the sacrificial fire, to the accompaniment of appropriate Vedic mantras; and (7) the disposal of the ritual implements by sacrificer's wife, while the priest pours an oblation in the fire.

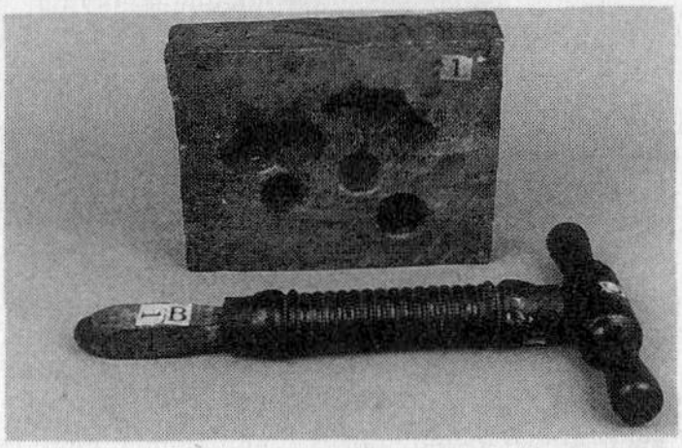

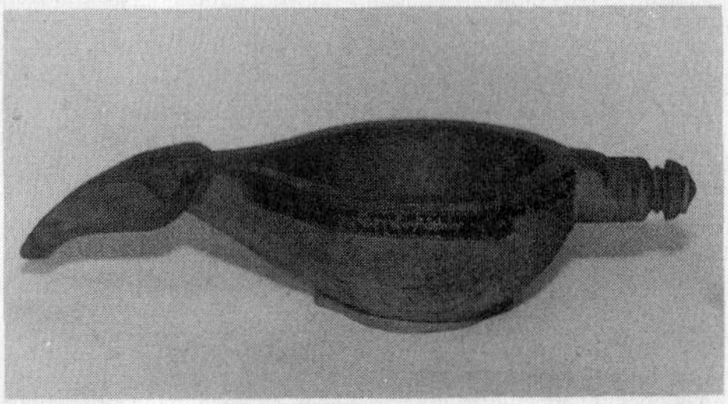

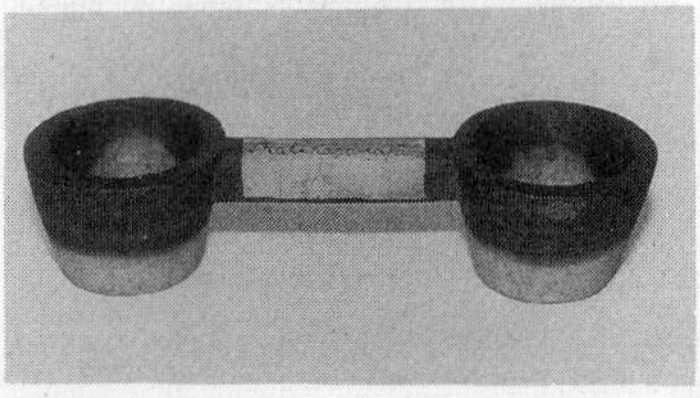

8–16. Vedic ritual implements. (*Twentieth century; collectors: James A. Santucci and Pitt Rivers Museum, Oxford.*) (8) Water bowl (left), used to receive purified water, and bowl for holding soma juice (right). (9) Fire kindler, including the lower kindler (top), upper kindler (rod and end piece), and secondary churner (handle). Fire is generated from the friction of two pieces of wood rubbed together (illustrated in number 3 above). (10) Mortar, used for pounding grains for oblations. (11) Womb-shaped ladle, used for offering oblations. (12) Sword, used to stir offering or to trim and shape the mount of the altar. (13) Ladle for offering oblation of clarified butter mixed with coagulated milk. (14) Bowl for holding the Brāhmaṇ's portion of the oblation. (15) (First) ladle (top) for offering solid or liquid oblations, and (second) ladle for oblations. The two are used in sequence to prevent mixing of offerings. (16). Vessel for separating grain from husks, used to keep two parts of oblation from mixing together.

17. Śiva Dakṣiṇāmūrti (The Lord Who Faces South). (*South India, twentieth century; collector: James A. Santucci.*) When Śiva appears in this position, it represents the manifestation of the god as a teacher or as the divinity of death.

18. Śiva Ardhanārīśvara (The Lord Whose Half Is a Woman) with Nandī. (*South India, twentieth century; collector: James A. Santucci.*) When Śiva appears in this position, it represents the god as the unity of both the male (Śiva) and female (Śakti) powers. Here he is depicted as riding on his vehicle, the bull Nandī.

19. Śiva Ardhanārīśvara (The Lord Whose Half Is a Woman). (*South India, nineteenth–twentieth century; collector: James A. Santucci.*) See illus. 18. Here Śiva is depicted without his vehicle, the bull Nandī.

20. RĀSA-LĪLĀ (Kṛṣṇa dancing with the Gopīs). (*Kāṅgrā [North India], mid nineteenth century; collector: Ingrid Aall.*) In this scene the cowherd Lord is shown dancing with the milkmaids.

21. KṚṢṆA AND RĀDHĀ. (*Orissā [South India], twentieth century; collector: Ingrid Aall.*) In this scene the Lord is depicted with his consort Rādhā, surrounded by attendants.

22. VIṢṆU DESTROYING MADHU AND KAIṬABHA. (*Guler [North India] [?], eighteenth–nineteenth century; collector: Charles Craig.*) In this scene from the *Devīmāhātmya* Viṣṇu is shown vanquishing the two demonds Madhu and Kaiṭabha seated on the cosmic serpent Śeṣa in the cosmic ocean.

23. HANUMAT CARRYING RĀMA AND LAKṢMAṆA. (*Pahārī [North India] [?], nineteenth century; collector: Charles Craig.*) In this scene the monkey god is shown carrying the two brothers Rāma and Lakṣmaṇa.

24. CHINNASMASTĀ. (*Kāṅgrā [North India] [?], nineteenth century; collector: Charles Craig.*) In this scene of Hindu Tantrism, the female representation of the sixth Great Knowledge (Mahāvidyā) arises from a copulating couple symbolizing pure cosmic fertility.

न.गी.
१५७

ब्रह्मा मम योनिर्महद्ब्रह्म तस्मिन्गर्भं
दधाम्यहं सम्भवः सर्वभूतानां ततो
भवति भारत ॥ सर्वयोनिषु कौन्तेय
मूर्तयः सम्भवन्ति याः ॥ तासां ब्रह्ममह
द्योनिरहं बीज प्रदः पिता ॥ भ॥ सर्वे

अ॑५
४

रागे
१५७

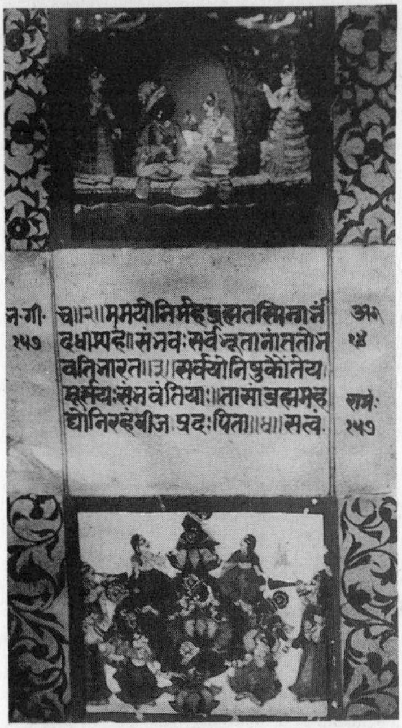

25. PASSAGE FROM THE *BHAGAVAD-
GĪTĀ*. (*Būndi School [North India],
nineteenth century; collector: Jane Wat-
son.*) This passage from *Bhagavad-gītā*
(14.3–4) is flanked on top and bottom
by scenes from the Rāsa-līlā (see illus.
20).

26. GAṄGĀ OR SARASVATĪ SEATED ON
A MYTHICAL BEAST. (*Kashmīr, nineteenth century; collector: Charles
Craig.*) In this scene the river goddess
Ganges or Sarasvatī (goddess of learning and speech) is riding on an unusual
sea monster.

27. VIṢṆU AND LAKṢMĪ ON ŚEṢA. (*Pahārī [North India], nineteenth century;
collector: Charles Craig.*) This scene depicts Viṣṇu and his wife Lakṣmī seated
on the cosmic serpent Śeṣa.

28. GAṆEŚA. (*Central India, twelfth century; collector: Robert Looker.*) This is the elephant-headed god, son of Śiva and Pārvatī, who is considered to be the remover of obstacles and the god of agriculture.

29. VIṢṆU. (*Location unknown, tenth century; collector: Charles Craig.*) This head depicts the benevolent, humanitarian god Viṣṇu.

Thus, if we take these passages at face value, the doctrine of transmigration was first promulgated by Yājñavalkya, who first divulged it only to one chosen disciple but later allowed it to become more or less public. The historicity of these passages, however, is at best dubious. They probably represent the teaching of Yājñavalkya, but the circumstances in which he taught them suggest the work of an editor endowed with considerable creativity.

Another key text on the origin of the doctrine of transmigration is contained in a later portion of the *Bṛhadāraṇyaka Upaniṣad* (6.2), obviously by another author from another source. It is repeated, with a few variations, in the second-oldest of the Upaniṣads, the *Chāndogya* (5.3–10). It concerns another famous sage, Uddālaka Āruṇi, of the *gotra* (brāhmaṇic kin group, or clan) of Gautama, and his son Śvetaketu. The latter, incidentally, figures in many of the accounts of Uddālaka's teaching as a rather obtuse young man, slow to understand the new doctrines evolved by his father and rather arrogant.

According to this account Śvetaketu once visited the assembly of the Pañcāla tribe, no doubt as a qualified brāhmaṇ, hoping to obtain largesse from them. A certain chieftain named Pravāhaṇa Jaivali noticed him. Jaivali, a *kṣatriya,* put a number of blunt questions to the young brāhmaṇ in an abrupt manner that did not indicate great respect: "Do you know how beings go away in different directions when they die? . . . Do you know how that world up there is not filled up by all the many souls that are constantly departing from here? . . . Do you know how to get to the Path of the Gods or the Path of the Fathers?"[12] Śvetaketu had to admit that, though he had been taught by his father all the brāhmaṇic lore, he could not answer one of these questions. Jaivali offered to teach him his secrets, but the young man was thoroughly offended at the thought of being instructed by a *kṣatriya* and hurried back to his father in annoyance. He told his father how the *kṣatriya* Jaivali had presumed to ask him questions he could not answer. Uddālaka, the father, could not answer them either, and he suggested to his son that they should both go and sit at the feet of the warrior chief and learn his new lore. The young man would not consent to do anything so humiliating, so the father went alone to Jaivali's court. The *kṣatriya* was at first disinclined to teach the brāhmaṇ, but the latter asked him so politely that he agreed, saying, "I hope you and your ancestors[13] won't do us any harm as a result of this. This wisdom has hitherto never been known by any brāhmaṇ, but who could refuse you when you ask so politely?" The teaching of Jaivali is rather too lengthy to quote verbatim, and much of it is not immediately relevant. It is summarized in what follows (*Chāndogya Upaniṣad* 5.5–10).

The birth of a child takes place as a result of a process interpreted as a series of sacrifices. In heaven the gods offer their faith and produce Soma (here a god, not a plant). In mid-space they offer Soma in the rain clouds, which are thought of as fiery because they contain lightning. On earth they offer the rain, and thus food is produced. In man they offer food, and semen is produced. In woman they offer the man's semen, and a child is produced. He lives his life and dies. Then his body "is carried off to the pyre, to go to the allotted place whence he came."

The souls of those who understand this mystery, as well as "those who in the forest revere faith as truth," merge in the flame of the pyre. After rather complicated peregrinations they reach the sun, and then in flashes of lightning, they are led to the World of Brahman. "For them there is no return."

The souls of the righteous dead who do not know the mystery, on the other hand, but who perform sacrifice, almsgiving, and penance, go through similar peregrinations and find their way to the World of the Fathers, the Āryan heaven. Thence, when their stock of merit is exhausted, they pass to the moon and "the gods eat them up." Thence they pass into space, from space to the wind, from the wind to the rain, and in the rain they come back to earth and "they turn into food." "Then they are again offered in the fire of man, then in the fire of women and then they are born to face these worlds once more; and so, over and over again, they are caught up in the cycle." This brief statement in the *Bṛhadāraṇyaka Upaniṣad* (6.2.16) is somewhat expanded and clarified in the *Chāndogya Upaniṣad* version (5.10.6): The soul, returning to earth in the rain, enters a plant. Ultimately the plant is eaten by a man or a male animal,[14] and the soul is transferred to a woman in his semen. Thus it is reborn as a living being.

The *Chāndogya* version adds a further passage (5.10.7–8): Those who have pleased the gods by their conduct are reborn in one of the three higher (twice-born) classes. Those whose conduct has been evil enter "a foul and stinking womb, such as that of a bitch, a pig or an outcaste." Small creatures like flies and worms do not enter either of the two paths. "Theirs is a third condition, to be born and die."

The doctrine of the *Bṛhadāraṇyaka Upaniṣad* appears again, in a much elaborated form, at the beginning of the early *Kauṣītaki Upaniṣad* (1.1–7). Here there are several striking differences. First, Uddālaka does not learn the doctrine from a warrior chief but from a certain Citra Gāṅgyāyani, who appears to have been another brāhmaṇ of the Gāṅgya *gotra*. The souls of all the dead go to the moon in the waxing half of its cycle and leave it again in its waning half. The moon asks the soul, "Who are you?" and if the right answer is not given, the soul returns to earth in the rain. The soul has to choose whether it wishes to return or go on further through the heavenly realms. Appropriate formulas are given, to be pronounced in the case of either choice. (This, incidentally, is perhaps the only passage in any Hindu scripture where it is considered that any being would positively wish to be reborn rather than fare onward to complete release from the burden of transmigration.) The final password to the higher realms is the answer to the moon's question, "Who are you?" the correct password being "I am you." This, however, is only the beginning of the soul's journey. It must undergo many tests and ordeals until at last it reaches the throne of the god Brahmā. Ultimately the soul identifies itself with Brahmā and is never again reborn.

These accounts of the doctrine of transmigration suggest that it began in narrow circles of the elite, not that it was widespread among the masses before it was taken up by the higher classes. It came as a new, rare, and almost secret doctrine. The two passages suggest that it began almost simultaneously among people who did not know one another. Since it was at first a new and secret doctrine it seems hardly likely that it was inspired by the beliefs of the non-Āryan indigenous inhabitants of the Ganges valley. One can suggest only that it arose out of floating ideas, which crystallized in similar form in the minds of more than one sage.

The more fantastic elements of Uddālaka's description of the process of transmigration may obscure the fact that in the context of time and place it was a brilliant hypothesis, answering simultaneously very important questions that must have greatly puzzled people of the time. It not only hypothesized the processes of birth, death, and rebirth but also accounted for the fact that, though people died in the millions for generation after generation, the World of the Fathers never became overcrowded. Also it explained why the moon waxed and waned. And finally it accounted for the remarkable fact that conception did not automatically follow intercourse—a child could be produced only if the male partner had eaten a vegetable containing the microscopic soul of a living being. We cannot but admire the sweep of Uddālaka's imagination.

If we accept the date of the *Bṛhadāraṇyaka Upaniṣad* most widely held by Western scholarship, about 650 B.C.E., we should not ignore the fact that ideas of transmigration were developing at the same time among the Greeks, coming to a head in the teaching of Pythagoras (born about 570 B.C.E.). Thus it was impossible for Greece to have taken the doctrine from India or India from Greece. Yet both civilizations devised similar doctrines at about the same time, though in Greece, unlike in India, transmigration never attained near universal acceptance. If there was any connection between the two doctrines it must have been through a common source in the Middle East. But we cannot trace such a source at present.

We have little or no evidence, moreover, of how the new doctrine of transmigration spread so as to be almost universally accepted within a century or two of its origin. In a later Upaniṣad, the *Kaṭha Upaniṣad* (1.20), the boy Naciketas asks a question of Yama, the god of death, which seems to indicate much uncertainty about the fate of the soul when the body has perished:

> . . . When a man is dead, there is this doubt.
> Some say, "He is," some say, "He is not."
> I want you to instruct me in this matter.

Evidently at the time this was composed some people were declaring that there was no life after death, and when a man died he was done for. Unfortunately we cannot date the text with certainty, but it seems to be at least a century later than the *Bṛhadāraṇyaka Upaniṣad* and probably more.

The reply of the god forms the substance of the Upaniṣad. With many analogies and figures of speech, in beautiful verse, Yama declares the secret of life after death. The very kernel of the human being is the self or soul (*ātman*). This self is the owner of, and passenger in, the chariot of the body. Its chrioteer is *buddhi,* a difficult word to translate, perhaps here meaning consciousness, awareness.[15] *Manas,* generally translated as mind, the sixth sense, which coordinates the other five,[16] according to Hindu theory, forms the reins, while the senses are the horses. To achieve the highest state, the *buddhi,* through the mind, must learn to control the vicious refractory senses, and

> He who always lacks discrimination, unmindful, impure, does not reach that [highest state] and goes [back] into the cycle (*saṃsāra*).

> But he who is always discriminating, mindful and pure, he reaches that state from which he will not be born again.[17]

There is here no question of transmigration being a secret doctrine, for at the end of the chapter (3.17)—which was probably originally the end of the text, other material being added later—we are told:

> He who proclaims this supreme mystery in an assembly of brāhmaṇs, or especially at the time of the performance of rites for the ancestors (*śrāddha*), he is fit for infinity; he is fit for infinity.

Thus transmigration is a fact of all life. It is, as is the case in all later assessments of it, a thoroughly undesirable state. The process is still something of a mystery, but the mystery has become an open secret and those who hear the Upaniṣad are encouraged to proclaim it, if not to all and sundry at least to the twice-born who might be present at the family ancestral ceremonies of *śrāddha,* which concluded with feasting.

The preceding passage suggests that the doctrine of transmigration was taught by the brāhmaṇs and filtered down to the lower orders. Another class of people who may have had a hand in spreading it was that of the ascetics and mystics, who became increasingly numerous as time went on. Many of these wandered about and taught whoever wished to hear, irrespective of class. In any case, by the time of the composition of the earliest scriptures of Buddhism, perhaps even by the time of the Buddha himself, the doctrine was accepted by everyone in the Ganges valley, as far as we can see, except by a small sect of materialists or Epicureans, led by a certain Ajita Keśakambalin, who maintained that there was no life whatever after death. An undercurrent of scepticism and unbelief continued in later times, in the school of thought referred to by orthodox Hindu, Buddhist, and Jain texts as Cārvāka, Lokāyata, or Nāstika.

FOUR

The Mystical and Ascetic Traditions

The Orthodox Movements

The doctrine of transmigration furthered the development of asceticism, and among the ascetics schools of mystics arose striving to achieve a sense of complete release from the trammels of the world. This movement was not a by-product of the doctrine of transmigration, though the latter may have encouraged its growth. Among the sayings attributed to Yājñavalkya, who was apparently one of the earliest proponents of the doctrine of transmigration, we find in the *Bṛhadāraṇyaka Upaniṣad* the following very important passage. It formed part of the long sermon that Yājñavalkya preached to King Janaka, in which he is said to have introduced the doctrine of transmigration for the first time in public, with the beautiful similes of the caterpillar and the goldsmith.[1] Later (4.4.22) the sage reverts to a theme that he has already touched on many times before: the self (*ātman*).

> That is the great unborn self, made of understanding (*vijñāna*) among the breaths, the space (*ākāśa*)[2] within the heart. In that rests the subduer of all [or of the universe], the lord of all, the king of all. He is no greater through good actions and no smaller

> through evil actions. He is the lord of all, he is the king of beings, he is the guardian of beings, he is the embankment, the support (*vidharaṇa*) of these worlds, so that they may not break up. The brāhmaṇs strive to know him by reciting the Vedas, by sacrifices, by almsgiving, by self-mortification (*tapas*), and by fasting, and when [a brāhmaṇ] knows him he becomes an advanced ascetic (*muni*).
>
> Wanderers wander forth desiring this as their world. This [self within the individual] is indeed that [absolute world spirit]! So, before that [spirit], wise men do [did] not desire progeny. What shall we do with progeny, [they say] when this self, this world, is ours. So they rise above their longing for sons, their longing for wealth, and their longing for [heavenly] worlds and they roam about as beggars. For longing for sons is [like] longing for wealth, longing for wealth is [like] longing for [heavenly] worlds—these are mere longing.
>
> The Self is "no, no." Impalpable, it is not grasped; indestructible, it is not destroyed; without contact, it does not cling [to anything], it is not bound, it does not tremble, it does not suffer (*riṣyati*). These two [thoughts] do not pass over [the mind of] him [who knows this]—"Hence I have done evil," and "hence I have done good." He passes over them. What he has done and what he has not done do not distress him.

The purport of much of this passage is repeated in many other places in the Upaniṣads. First of all, it reflects the growth of asceticism, of "giving up the world." Earlier ascetics, it appears, were generally elderly hermits (*vānaprastha*), living in the forests, but here we have another type of ascetic, the wanderer (*parivrājaka*). Ideally the motive for their asceticism was no longer to gain supernatural power or expunge sins by penance but to search inwardly for an absolute and final entity, the Great Unborn Self who dwelt in the heart of every being but who had to be realized by meditation and ascetic praxis. This self was finally identical with Brahman, the absolute being that was behind the phenomenal world and on which the phenomenal world depended. The identity of the *ātman*, the individual self, and Brahman, the world spirit, is proclaimed time and again with an immense number of similes and metaphors throughout the Upaniṣadic literature, but with significant variations.

Throughout the history of Hinduism, from the time of the Upaniṣads down to the present day, there has been much controversy as to whether the absolute and ultimate entity is "without characteristics" (*nirguṇa*) or "with characteristics" (*saguṇa*). The earlier seers seem on the whole to have favoured the first alternative; yet they could not avoid personifying the impersonal world spirit in which they believed. So, in the above passage, the great unborn self is masculine and is given the characteristics of a mighty ruler—of God, in fact. Yet in other passages Yājñavalkya refers to the same entity in the neuter gender, not as a personal god but as an impersonal essence (3.8.8, 9, 11).

> This indeed . . . is what brāhmaṇs call the Imperishable. It is not coarse or fine, not short or long . . . without shadow, without darkness, without wind, without space (*ākāśa*), without attachment, without flavour or fragrance, without eye or ear, without speech or mind, without face or measure, without inside or outside. It consumes nothing and nobody consumes it. . . .
>
> Sun and moon, heaven and earth, the moments and [the measures of time up to] the year, all these are held apart and remain apart at the order of the Imperishable, from the white mountains some rivers flow east and others run west, each in its own direction at the order of the Imperishable. At the order of the Imperishable, men praise the generous givers. At the order of the Imperishable the gods depend on the sacrifices and the ancestors on the rites for the dead. . . .
>
> That Imperishable is the unseen seer, the unheard hearer, the unthought thinker, the ununderstood understander. There is no seer, no hearer, no thinker, no understander other than . . . this Imperishable. In this Imperishable the warp and woof of space is woven.

Here, though Yājñavalkya refers to the absolute *Brahman* largely in negative terms (*neti, neti,* "no, no" "not that, not that" in the earlier passage), he cannot but give it positive functions, as the weaver by whom space is woven, the ordainer of the cosmos, the unseen seer, and so on. He finds it very difficult to conceive an absolute without some degree of personification. Later, with the development of schools of philosophy, learned men were able to conceive a truly impersonal Brahman, but in the early Upaniṣads the absolute, despite its neuter gender, has invariably some degree of personality.

Yājñavalkya's teaching about the self (*ātman*) and the absolute Brahman is by no means abstract. Knowledge of the Brahman, moreover, brings almost unmeasurable bliss (4.3.33). The wise man must so train himself that his soul realizes its full identity with Brahman. Then it will not be reborn but will enjoy the immense bliss of Brahman forever. This training toward identity is often referred to in some later sources as the Way of Knowledge (*jñānamārga*) and so it is, but the knowledge is not intellectual knowledge but knowledge from acquaintance, like the knowledge a man has of his wife (or vice versa) multiplied by infinity. The general purport of the teaching ascribed to Yājñavalkya, however, is of an ultimate absolute that, on final analysis, is without gender, personality, or distinctive characteristics—in fact, the *nirguṇa-Brahman* of later Vedāntic philosophy.

But Yājñavalkya's was not the only view, and within the *Bṛhadāraṇyaka Upaniṣad* itself we can find sharp contrasts. The first sections of the Upaniṣad contain interesting and significant accounts of the creation or evolution of the cosmos. These mutually inconsistent legends are not ascribed to Yājñavalkya. Rather, the seers who thought out these stories are unknown; and they show a very wide range of speculation.

In *Bṛhadāraṇyaka Upaniṣad* (1.2), we are told that in the beginning nothing existed but Death, identified with Hunger. After producing the elements and space Death "longed for a second self" and produced the Year. The first inclination of Death and

Hunger was to eat up his firstborn son, but he decided against it, thinking "If I should eat him I should make my food less!" So Death created the whole world and all that it contains, including humans, as food for himself.

This strange and macabre myth implies, in demythologized terms, that everything is destroyed by time. Whatever comes into being is bound to perish, to provide food for Death. The passage, in fact, anticipates the basic doctrine of Buddhism, that all things without exception pass away. The mythologizing language tends to blur the fundamentally philosophic character of this legend. Moreover, the story gives us an impersonal interpretation of the cosmos as controlled by a mysterious power that produces only for the sake of destroying its own products.

An impersonal universe is similarly described in another passage from the *Bṛhadāraṇyaka Upaniṣad* (1.4.10), which commences "In the beginning this [universe] was Brahman"—the neuter impersonal absolute. But the first event of cosmic evolution was its knowledge of its self, and *self* is masculine. This is a foretaste of the view of the Advaita Vedānta school of philosophy, which holds that the ultimate absolute is impersonal, but that the first emanation from that impersonal entity was a personality, in the form of the High God. And the Advaitins tend to disparage the theists, who have only reached the purlieus, so to speak, of Ultimate Bliss in their insistence that a personal God (whether Viṣṇu or Śiva) is ultimate.

On the other hand, in the same chapter of the *Bṛhadāraṇyaka Upaniṣad* (1.4.1 ff.) we read, "In the beginning this [universe] was the self (*ātman*) alone, in the form of a male person (*puruṣa*)." This passage, conveniently overlooked by many later monists, is quite explicit and admits of no alternative translation. At the back of all things is a personal God. The legend goes on to relate that the primal person felt lonely; so he divided himself into two and produced a female counterpart. From the mating of the primeval pair all living beings were born.

We refer to these new accounts of the origin of all things to show the richness and variety of the Upaniṣadic literature. Here, one after the other, we meet three legends, ascribing primacy to Death, Brahman, and a personal self respectively. These divergent myths of creation are paralleled by many other passages in the Upaniṣads and other ancient Indian religious texts, in which one passage seems to negate another that went before. There is no means of harmonizing such passages, though nearly all the early and many later commentators have attempted to do so. We must simply accept the fact that there was much difference of opinion among the mystics and ascetics who compiled the Upaniṣads, and the final redactor of the *Bṛhadāraṇyaka Upaniṣad* preferred to give a number of points of view, leaving it to qualified listeners to decide which of them corresponded most closely with their own insights.

We have no space to discuss in detail the contents of the twelve or thirteen early Upaniṣads.[3] On the basis of content, language, and style they have been tentatively ranged in chronological order, but their dates are still very uncertain. The beautiful *Śvetāśvatara Upaniṣad,* composed in verse, deserves mention, however, because it is explicitly theist or indeed monotheist and is devoted to glorifying the god Rudra, occasionally referred to in the text by his later name, Śiva. The impersonal Brahman is subordinate, an emanation of Śiva himself (6.1).

Some sages say "Inherent Nature,"
Others say "Time" [is the first cause], and both are wrong.
No—it is the glory of God in the world
That starts and turns the wheel of Brahmā.

The theology of the *Śvetāśvatara Upaniṣad* differs little from that of the *Bhagavad-gītā,* except that Śiva does not here become incarnate on earth, as Viṣṇu does in his *avatāras*. The two texts may not be very far apart in time, for it must be remembered that the *Bhagavad-gītā* is referred to as an Upaniṣad in the epic from which it is taken.

The Heterodox Movements

In the sixth century B.C.E. there was something of a rapid advance in the culture of the Ganges valley. It is marked by the appearance of more small cities, a fine new type of pottery with a lustrous black polish, coined money, and probably writing.[4] The centre of cultural change was Magadha, that part of the present-day state of Bihār south of the Ganges River and north of the hills, but in other parts of the Ganges area there was also marked progress. The kings of Magadha were enterprising. Their kingdom was to grow over the centuries to become the mightiest empire of ancient India—indeed the mightiest in the world at that time.

Among the wandering ascetics new ideas fermented. Many of them travelled in groups, begging their way from village to village, teaching whoever wished to listen and arguing vigorously with their rivals. Some of the wanderers gave up all connection with the Vedas and the brāhmaṇ priesthood and opposed their doctrines and practices root and branch. There was even one movement led by a certain Ajita Keśakambalin (Ajita of the Hair-blanket, referring perhaps to the dress of his order) which rejected the immaterial and supernatural altogether and preached thoroughgoing materialism.

> "Man," he said, "is formed of the four elements. When he dies earth returns to the aggregate of earth, water to water, fire to fire, and air to air, while his senses vanish into space. Four men with bier take up the corpse; they gossip [about the dead man] as far as the burning-ground, where his bones turn the colour of a dove's wing and his sacrifices end in ashes. They are fools who preach almsgiving, and those who maintain the existence [of immaterial categories] speak vain and lying nonsense. When the body dies both fool and wise alike are cut off and perish. They do not survive after death."[5]

Many of the teachers, both the hermits and the wanderers, appear to have rapidly accepted the doctrine of transmigration, and it was probably mainly through them that it reached the general public. Certain corollaries of the doctrines were made much of by the heterodox ascetics. For one thing, the doctrine included animals as well as humans, god, and demons in the scheme of *saṃsāra*.[6] Thus the dividing line between animal, human, demonic, and divine was somewhat blurred. It was always possible for a human being in one life to become an animal in the next. Thus the soul of one's grandfather might at this moment be inhabiting the body of a monkey or an ox. The conclusion was obvious: The wanton killing of animals is little better than murder, and meat eating is little better than cannibalism. Thus, from that time to this, respectable Indians have been inclined to vegetarianism. The new ideas gave currency to a new word, *ahiṃsā,* nonviolence, which was to have a long history, down to the present day.

The more orthodox brāhmaṇs and ascetics made an exception as far as sacrifice was concerned. In the *Chāndogya Upaniṣad* (8.15) we are told that the brāhmaṇ man who fulfills his religious obligation, who has concentrated all his senses on the *ātman,* the self, and who injures no living thing except in the ritual of sacrifices[7] will not be reborn but will pass on death straight to the World of Brahman (*Brahmaloka*).

It seems that there were always groups of thaumaturges and medicine men on the fringe of orthodoxy, who may have been much respected by some of the public. The *Ṛg-veda* tells us of the *munis,* a class of shamans associated with the god Rudra, capable of magical feats and apparently respected and sometimes feared. Somewhat later, in the *Atharva-veda,* we meet the *vrātyas,* possibly one of the prototypes of the Gypsies who migrated to Europe in the Middle Ages. These people wandered from place to place in small groups, led by a chief. They carried their property in carts and included in their number musicians and prostitutes. They performed rituals of a magical type, which sometimes included flagellation, and like the *munis* they were much respected by the populace. They were outside Āryan society, and it appears that the brāhmaṇs made considerable efforts to incorporate them into the orthodox social order.[8]

The sixth century B.C.E. saw the appearance of numerous ascetic movements that completely rejected the Vedas, the sacrificial cult that the Vedas taught, and the authority of the brāhmaṇs who performed the sacrifices. In general, the new movements were antiritualistic. All, however, except presumably the materialists who followed Ajita Keśakambalin, accepted the truth of transmigration and the advisability of escaping from the cycle of rebirth. But they rejected all ideas of creation, whether by a personal God or by an impersonal absolute. For them the universe was the product solely of natural law and went through unending cycles of advance and decline according to natural law. All the new sects, as far as we can see, aimed at releasing their members from the bonds of birth, death, and rebirth by the quickest method. This, they believed, could be achieved only by the complete renunciation of all worldly ties, by owning nothing, or next to nothing, and by devoting all one's time to spiritual activities. Among the most potent causes of evil *karman*, binding humans to the cycle of rebirth, were acts of violence, especially killing. The ascetic must do everything in his power to avoid even the accidental killing of any creature whatever.

The leaders of the new heterodox sects claimed great antiquity for their doctrines and movements, looking back to former leaders; but it is doubtful if there is much basis for their claims. In an early Indian context, especially, the legitimization of religiophilosophical movements such as these depended on establishing their antiquity, and this could be done only by claiming to reproduce the doctrines of sages of the ancient past. The former Buddhas and former *Tīrthaṅkaras* (of Jainism) have no reliable historical basis, for no earlier ascetic movements of this type are attested anywhere either in the Vedic literature or by archaeology. We do not believe in the existence of earlier śramaṇic movements in the Ganges valley. This was a new development in the religious life of India, which had its roots not in the śramaṇic movements but in the sages of the Upaniṣads.

We know the names of several heterodox leaders, but only three made a lasting impact on Indian religious life. Undoubtedly the most important was Siddhārtha Gautama, known by his followers as Buddha, the Awakened One.[9] Buddha founded a world religion, but his doctrines need not long detain us here.[10] As far as we can reconstruct its beliefs, the earliest Buddhist community taught a rather pessimistic phenomenalism and dynamism. All objects, all phenomena, are composite, made up of a number of changing factors, psychological and physical. There is no self or soul, in the sense of the personality that is constantly the same in all phenomenal changes; but a complex chain of cause and effect keeps the specious personality alive and carries it over from one life to the next. Thus Buddhism, though it rejects the existence of the soul, accepts the doctrine of rebirth.

The cycle of birth, life, death, and rebirth is kept going by the thirst (*taṅhā*) or craving of the individual. The cycle is essentially unpleasant and painful (*dukkha*), and to escape from it one must give up desire, cease to want anything, and accept the inevitable passing away of all phenomenal things. The ultimate state is looked on as a calmly blissful condition from which all personality has vanished; it is essentially indescribable, a state that cannot be fully understood by the ordinary person. It is known as *nirvāṇa,* blowing out, the extinguishing of rebirth.

The doctrine of the Buddha was propagated by an order (*saṅgha*) of yellow-robed monks, probably the world's first disciplined monastic order. Their rules were not so strict as those of most other heterodoxies, but their way of life was austere enough. They were required to beg their daily food and hence were known as beggars (*bhikkhu*). They were forbidden to eat after midday. At first they moved constantly from place to place, but this was impossible in the rainy season, when they gathered in temporary huts or caves, which later evolved into monasteries. Their number and influence increased greatly from the time of Aśoka, who was converted to Buddhism and vigorously promoted the growth of the religion. It was in Aśoka's day that Buddhism began to become an international religion with the conversion of King Devānampiya Tissa of Śrī Laṅkā and many of his courtiers and subjects. There is evidence of occasional animosity against Buddhism and mild persecution of Buddhism by orthodox rulers, but in general the faiths lived side by side without much friction.

Jainism—centring on the teachings of Vardhamāna, who was called Mahāvīra (Great Hero), with the additional titles of *Jina* (Conqueror) and *Tīrthaṅkara* (Ford-maker over the river of the world)—was more extreme than Buddhism in most of its tenets. According to the Jain tradition, Mahāvīra formed an order on the basis of an earlier group of ascetics, introducing as an innovation the rule of strict nakedness at all times and complete abstinence from all sexual activity. The basic doctrine of Jainism is hylozoism—the belief that all things whatever, including fire and water, wind and earth and stones, are alive. There is an infinite number of souls, called in Jainism *jīvas* (lives), in the universe, each burdened with a load of matter in varying degrees. The gods in heaven have very light bodies through which the soul can display a little of its intrinsic radiance. The soul in the stone on the roadside, on the other hand, is so heavily pressed down by matter that its presence can hardly be suspected, but it is there nevertheless, essentially the equal of the soul of the god. Souls carry over their load of *karman* to the next life and find a body consistent with their *karman*.

The lower forms of life have no power of will or decision and therefore they cannot acquire new *karman*, but they must wait very long periods until much of the bad *karman* they have acquired has worn away before they are reborn in a higher state. Only human beings and some of the higher animals have the power to affect their own *karman;* thus they can work their way higher in the scale of existence by disciplined behaviour, designed to insure that as little as possible of evil *karman* enters the body, and by voluntarily undertaking hardships and austerities of one kind or another, in order to get rid of the evil *karman* clouding over the soul. When the soul is finally liberated its natural lightness carries it to the top of the universe, above the highest heaven, where it remains in bliss for all eternity, in its natural state, mirroring the universe in an eternal act of omniscient perception.[11] In their insistence on the infinite number of eternal souls that are entirely separate from one another, Jainism is diametrically opposed to many other Indian systems of thought, which tend to reduce all apparent distinctions to an ultimate unity. For the Jains the aim of the spiritual quest is not union but isolation.

The most dangerous source of evil *karman,* for the Jain, is violence to other living things. Conscious and intentional acts of violence obviously bring much evil *karman* in their wake, but even unconscious acts such as carelessly treading on an insect in one's path are serious enough; and in view of the fact that all things are live, the soul intent on complete salvation must be doubly careful. Of course there is a hierarchy of life, from stones upward, and injury to lower beings is less serious than to higher ones, but to pick up a stone and throw it into a pool is likely to harm the stone, the air through which it flies, and the water of the pool, and thus to perform such an act for no good reason is not commendable. Of all the religions of India, Jainism most stresses *ahiṃsā.*

The Jain monk's discipline, therefore, is extremely strict. He must walk slowly and circumspectly to avoid treading on insects. He cannot light a fire or a lamp in his monastery, for thus injury would be done not only to the air but also to numerous insects. Originally he might own no property whatever but wander naked through the villages, begging his food by silently holding out his cupped hands. He was expected to undertake numerous fasts and ultimately, when his faculties began to fail in old age, to fast to death by slow stages.

Obviously lay Jains could not subject themselves to such strict discipline, but they were expected to follow the rule of *ahiṃsā* as far as possible. They were especially forbidden to take up professions that involved injury to life. Soldiers, hunters, and butchers were not accepted as Jain laymen without giving up their professions, and many other professions were also excluded. The farmer injures the oxen by forcing them to pull heavy carts and farm implements; he injures worms and innumerable other insects in the earth in his agricultural operations; he injures his crops by cutting them and the weeds in his fields by pulling them up; he injures the earth itself by digging, ploughing, and harrowing it. Though most of the injuries committed by the farmer are inflicted on beings very low in the scale of life, they are serious enough. Trades that appear quite innocuous to us involve, for the Jain, serious injury to insentient beings. When a tree is cut down the injured soul of the tree is left behind in the stump, but the felled tree immediately becomes the home of earth souls that are born in the dead timber. These suffer unimaginable agony as the branches are lopped off and the trunk sawn up into planks and later when the planks are nailed together. Thus carpentry is not a suitable profession for a good Jain—and the same is true of almost any other craft.

In fact trade is almost the only possible profession for the lay Jain, and for over two thousand years most Jains have generally been successful businessmen, with a reputation for fair dealing and honesty, and over the centuries many Jain families have become very rich. They are famous for their good works—for their endowment not only of Jain temples and monasteries but also of hospitals for people and animals and of educational and charitable establishments of all kinds for the benefit of non-Jains as well as coreligionists.

The Jains suffered a great schism beginning in about 300 B.C.E. One group held the view that in this age of cosmic decline the monastic community was compelled to give up certain of the stricter rules, such as the complete nakedness of the monks. The other group insisted on maintaining strict nudity. The first became known as Śvetāmbara (having white garments) and the second as Digambara (approximately, having space as their garments). The division persists to this day, the White-clad Jains predominating in Gujarāt and Rājasthān and the Space-clad in Kārnātaka (the latter, incidentally, have now compromised to some extent, and many of the monks wear garments when outside the monastery). Though the schism is very ancient and the two groups have different scriptures, their doctrines are essentially the same.

The Jains never successfully exported their doctrines to other parts of India, as did the Buddhists. At certain periods in some areas of India they appear to have been very widespread and influential, and great kings declared themselves lay Jains.[12] There are presently no more than about two million Jains in India, but their wealth and educational standards give them an influence much greater than their numbers would suggest.

One of the most surprising aspects of Jainism is the remarkable intellectual activity of Jain monks. Many of them became great scholars in many fields of learning, and many of the monasteries still contain large manuscript libraries, including books several centuries old. It was considered a work of merit for a Jain to copy a manuscript, even a secular one, and thus pass it on to posterity. Hence the Jains have preserved many texts that would otherwise have been completely lost. When we remember that the Jain monks carried out their intellectual work often on starvation rations, in monasteries without artificial light or heat, their achievement is doubly impressive.[13]

A third sect of considerable importance was that of the Ājīvikas,[14] founded by Makkhali Gosāla at about the same time as the foundation of Buddhism and Jainism. This sect has now completely disappeared and its scriptures have vanished with it. All we know about it is gathered from the prejudiced scriptures of its rivals, and thus our knowledge is fragmentary. It is clear, however, that the basic doctrine of Ājīvikism was fatalism. All phenomena and all processes in the universe were the effects of an impersonal force or power called *niyati,* and human free will was an illusion. The course of transmigration was, like everything else, rigidly fixed, and all beings went through an enormous series of rebirths until the last *niyati* brought them to a stage where they would become Ājīvika monks and ultimately achieve salvation.

> All that have breath, all that are born, all that have life, are without power, strength or virtue, but are developed by destiny, chance and nature, and experience joy and sorrow in the six classes [of existence]. There are . . . 8,400,000 great aeons, through which fool and wise alike must take their course and make an end of sorrow. There is no [question of] bringing in ripe karma[n] to fruition, nor of exhausting karma[n] already ripened by virtuous conduct, by vows, by penance, or by chastity. That cannot be done. Saṃsāra is measured as with a bushel, with its joy and sorrow and its appointed end. It can neither be lessened nor increased, nor is there any excess or deficiency of it. Just as a ball of string will, when thrown, unwind to its full length, so fool and wise alike will take their course, and make an end of sorrow.[15]

With this doctrine—to us, a depressing one—allowing no scope to human effort, it is perhaps not surprising that the Ājīvikas disappeared; but their leader, Makkhali Gosāla, was apparently a very important figure in the spiritual life of the period around 500 B.C.E., and the Ājīvikas remained a significant element in the religious life of the Ganges plain until the end of the Mauryan empire (about 300–185 B.C.E.). They survived in parts of Tamil Nādu until the fourteenth century.

Though the rise of the heterodox sects was unpopular with the brāhmaṇ pandits and the orthodox, the presence of three or four rival religious movements competing for the support of the laity was far less disruptive than one might expect. Though the heterodoxies might gain much support from certain laypersons, the brāhmaṇs always possessed one advantage that the heterodox sects lacked. In the rites of passage, such as birth, marriage, and death, the brāhmaṇs were the only priests who could perform the rituals correctly and ensure the spiritual security of the persons concerned. The Buddhists never took over this function from the brāhmaṇs, and it seems that Buddhist laypersons were always simultaneously in some measure Hindu laypersons. The same was largely true of the Jains, but Jains in later times managed to persuade certain brāhmaṇs to join their sect, and these brāhmaṇs evolved specially adapted domestic rituals for their Jain clients, whose worship was centred in the home or at temples.

There is a general view, largely inspired by Marxist theories on the relations of religious philosophy with the prevailing class system, that the rise of the heterodoxies such as Buddhism and Jainism was concomitant with the rise of an influential mercantile class that gave its support to these new movements, which were less expensive than orthodoxy and gave a greater place to the laity in religious activities. There may be some truth in this, but there were many other factors in the rise of these sects, and the idea that the main supporters of early Buddhism were well-to-do merchants is not wholly borne out by the evidence of the early Buddhist texts. Though many members of the middle classes gave support to Buddhism, it appears that brāhmaṇs formed the largest group of both the monks and the lay supporters of Buddhism.[16] Buddhism in its early form appealed chiefly to the intellectuals and rulers, and few members of the lower orders supported it.

One of the most important effects of the heterodox sects in the context of Hinduism is their opposition to animal sacrifice and their support of the doctrine of *ahiṃsā*. As a result of their steady pressure, such sacrifices became less and less frequent until they disappeared altogether. Later a different form of animal sacrifice arose, among the mediaeval sects devoted to Śiva's feminine aspect, Śakti, but the old Vedic sacrifices slowly came to an end. Doubts were early raised, even by the more orthodox teachers recorded in the Upaniṣads, as to the efficacy of sacrificial ritual in achieving more than temporal blessings. The heterodox teachers went further and completely condemned it. Steadily sentiment in favour of nonviolence spread. As far as laypersons were concerned, acts of violence were justified only in certain circumstances, such as in self-defense, in righteous warfare, and in the enforcement of law. The motive for nonviolence was not purely respect for life on a self-sacrificing ethical basis, but also enlightened self-interest. Once the doctrines of *karman* and *saṃsāra* were accepted, it was generally agreed by orthodox and heterodox alike that acts of violence were among the most potent sources of bad *karman*, leading to very unpleasant rebirths.

FIVE

Orthodoxy and the Epic Tradition

The period that followed the early Upaniṣadic sages and the birth of Buddhism and Jainism saw great changes in India. The small kingdom of Magadha (southern Bihār) gradually expanded until in the fourth century B.C.E. it controlled most of the Ganges plain. Toward the end of the sixth century B.C.E. the Achaemenian rulers of Irān conquered much of the northwest, at least as far as the Indus River; and in 326 B.C.E. the world-conquering Alexander of Macedon tried to found an empire in India but was compelled to retire without gaining permanent control even of the Indus area. The retreat of Alexander allowed for the rise of a new dynasty, the Mauryans, whose first ruler was Candragupta (about 320–296 B.C.E.), who at the time of his death was ruler of the greatest empire in the world at the time, ranging as it did from Afghānistān to Bengal. His successors added further to the kingdom, and the third emperor, Aśoka (about 270–232 B.C.E.), controlled all the subcontinent except the extreme south—the largest empire in South Asia until the nineteenth century.

The Mauryans appear to have been upstarts, members not of the brāhmaṇic, or priestly, class but of the *kṣatriya*, or princely, order. They seem to have favoured the heterodoxies, and Aśoka became a Buddhist. It was probably due to his patronage that Buddhism became so important. The Mauryans declined and fell, giving way to the Śuṅgas, whose founder was a brāhmaṇ general who performed the horse sacrifice.

To find an approprite chronological niche for the two great epics of India in this time of changing events is almost impossible: For one thing, we do not know their dates, and for another their composition covered a very long period. They contain remembrances of events that may have taken place almost a thousand years before Christ; and at the same time there is evidence of much later retouching—in the case of the *Mahābhārata* perhaps as late at 500 C.E.

After the four Vedas, with their annexed Brāhmaṇas, Āraṇyakas, and Upaniṣads, other texts associated with the Vedas were composed; these were the *Kalpa Sūtras,*[1] brief texts on ritual, ethics, and law. Theoretically, a *Kalpa Sūtra* is divided into three parts: *Śrauta Sūtra,* dealing with sacrificial ritual; *Gṛhya Sūtra,* dealing with domestic rituals and rites of passage; and *Dharma Sūtra,* dealing with morals, ethics, law, and politics. In fact each text of the three groups, attributed to an ancient sage, must be looked on as a separate composition. These texts were mostly worked over later, but their kernel goes back to around 500 B.C.E., at least in some cases.

Indian religious literature falls into two broad classes. The most holy and oldest is *śruti,* "that which is heard." This includes all the Vedic literature from the four Vedas to the Upaniṣads which are sometimes called Vedānta, or the "End of the Vedas." Texts appended to the Vedas, like the *Kalpa Sūtras* and other specialized texts on metrics, chants, and so on, are in a class by themselves called Vedāṅgas, or Appendages to the Vedas. The second great class of religious literature is *smṛti,* "that which is remembered," not so directly inspired as *śruti* but of varying sanctity.

Smṛti par excellence is the series of versified legal and ethical texts, developing from the *Dharma Sūtras,* known as *Dharma Śāstras* or simply *smṛti* (thus the *Dharma Śāstra* ascribed to the sage Manu is often commonly known as *Manu Smṛti*). These texts began to be composed only around the beginning of the common era.

There was also another branch of *smṛti,* known as Itihāsa-Purāṇa. *Itihāsa,* a peculiar Sanskrit compound noun from the words for "thus (*iti*) indeed (*ha*) it was (*āsa*)," is conventionally translated as history, and it has this meaning in the modern languages of India. In its original context it implies legends about kings and sages believed to have lived in the remote past. *Purāṇa* means ancient and the Purāṇas are collections of legends, myths, and moral precepts, orally transmitted up to the time of writing. There are eighteen principal Purāṇas, containing much ancient lore, but none of them appeared in its present form until well into our own era. Here we consider the two voluminous works classed as Itihāsa, the great epics of India, the *Mahābhārata* and the *Rāmāyaṇa.*

Of the two the *Mahābhārata* contains the oldest material, but there is good reason to believe that the text, even that of the critical edition,[2] was brought up to date as late as about 500 C.E.[3] Some of the narrative verses, on the other hand, may have been composed over a thousand years earlier than this. The poem in fact consists of a narrative in verse, into which have been interpolated many later passages, some of great length. Many of these interpolations are also narratives, but others are purely didactic and religious. The most famous and important of such interpolations is the *Bhagavad-gītā.* The longest is the *Śānti Parvan;* it and the following *Anuśāsana Parvan* form the twelfth and thirteenth of the eighteen books (*parvan*) of the epic. These two books, running to about twenty thousand verses, are in fact a lengthy anthology of early Hindu doctrinal and ethical passages. Among the numerous stories sandwiched into the narrative of the great epic are several that became part of the folklore of India—such as the tales of Nala and Damayantī (3.52–79), Śakuntalā (1.68–72), Sāvitrī (2.293–99), and Rāma, the hero of the other great epic, the *Rāmāyaṇa* (3.273–76). Some recensions of the *Mahābhārata* run to nearly a hundred thousand verses, mostly of thirty-two syllables each, making this the longest poem in the world, and even the Pūṇe critical edition, which omits many passages interpolated in later times, contains about seventy thousand verses.

When shorn of its interpolations, the *Mahābhārata* tells a stirring story of family rivalry and war. Many books on Hindu mythology or legend give a full summary of the story. The conflict concerns two sets of cousins: the Pāṇḍavas, or the five sons of Paṇḍu (Yudhiṣṭhira, Bhīma, Arjuna, Nakula, and Sahadeva), and the Kauravas (descendants of Kuru), the one hundred sons of the blind Dhṛtarāṣṭra, the eldest of whom was Duryodhana. Both sets of cousins claim the throne of the Kuru land, with its capital at Hastināpura, about fifty-five miles (ninety kilometres) northeast of modern Delhi. At first it was agreed to divide the kingdom, and the Pāṇḍavas made their capital at Indraprastha, near modern Delhi, though they had the legal right to the whole kingdom. In a great gambling contest between the two sets of cousins the eldest of the Pāṇḍavas, Yudhiṣṭhira, foolishly staked and lost his whole property, including Draupadī, the common wife of the five brothers—a strange feature of the story, apparently looking back to the very ancient time when polyandry was socially acceptable. The old King Dhṛtarāṣṭra forced his sons to return Draupadī, but the brothers were driven into exile for thirteen years. After that time they returned. They found numerous allies, as indeed the Kauravas did, and both sides prepared for battle. The Pāṇḍavas were advised by Kṛṣṇa—king of Mathurā and son of Vāsudeva and Devakī—who became their mentor and served as charioteer to Arjuna in the battle.

When the battle was over, none of the combatants remained alive but the five Pāṇḍavas. Yudhiṣṭhira became king of the Kuru realm and, aided by his brothers, ruled wisely and justly for many years. The last two books may be a later addition, for they show a more advanced ethic, influenced by the doctrine of *ahiṃsā*. They describe Yudhiṣṭhira's abdication and the journey of the five brothers and Draupadī to the Himālayas to find heaven.

The traditional author of the *Mahābhārata* is held by most Indians to be the sage Kṛṣṇa Dvaipāyana Vyāsa, who, according to the introduction to the epic, taught his poem to his pupil Vaiśampāyana. The latter in turn recited the complete work in public for the first time at the great snake sacrifice of King Janamejaya, the great-grandson of Arjuna, a hero of the epic. From that point, it was transmitted orally for all subsequent generations to enjoy.[4]

The story as just outlined has nothing particularly religious about it, except in the last two books. Divested of its didactic interpolations, it is essentially a tale of vicissitudes, heroic deeds, treachery, and loyalty, comparable to the great martial epics of Europe, such as the *Iliad* and the *Nibelungenlied*. Evidently the *Mahābhārata* began as such a poem and was later taken over by the brāhmaṇs and converted into a religious text. We have no positive evidence of how or why this was done, and we can only make suggestions.

In the course of the horse sacrifice (*aśvamedha*) and certain other lengthy Vedic sacrifices, brāhmaṇs would recite to the populace stories, especially connected with the ancestors of the king who was sponsoring the sacrifice. One can conceive that the story of the great war became particularly popular, and many kings, even though not direct descendants of the Pāṇḍava heroes, would find some remote or fictitious relationship which would give them a claim to connect the theme of this poem with their families. Thus the *Mahābhārata* became increasingly popular with both the ruling class and the masses. The brāhmaṇs more and more took it over from the royal bards who were originally responsible for its transmission. As they did so they incorporated many doctrinal, mythological, and theological passages, often rather crudely sandwiched into the main narrative, until it became an enormous encyclopaedia of early Hinduism. Judging from various references in the text itself and other evidence, we believe that one particular brāhmaṇic clan, or *gotra,* the Bhārgavas, may have had a special hand in the enlargement and further transmission of the poem.

The hero Kṛṣṇa, friend and mentor of the Pāṇḍavas, had a brilliant future ahead of him as the most important incarnation of Viṣṇu, but he has no such status in most of the epic. It is very possible that in its earliest form the story of the war of the Pāṇḍavas and the Kauravas contained no Kṛṣṇa whatever, for he is not essential to the plot.

According to tradition the great battle took place about 3000 B.C.E., when archaeologists declare that agriculture had barely begun in the northwest of the subcontinent. If there is any historical basis whatever to the story of the war, it must have occurred around the very beginning of the first millennium B.C.E.[5] On the other hand, in the *Chāndogya Upaniṣad* Kṛṣṇa, son of Devakī, appears as a wise teacher of a doctrine that has some features of the doctrine of selfless action in the *Bhagavad-gītā.* This latter Kṛṣṇa cannot have lived long before the composition of the Upaniṣad, generally dated around 650 B.C.E. Thus the Upaniṣad's Kṛṣṇa, son of Devakī, was not contemporary with the great battle, in which case he cannot have figured in the story in its oldest form.

In the narrative part of the *Mahābhārata* we find reflections of the life of the western part of the Ganges plain in the earlier part of the first millennium B.C.E. We find there a patchwork of small kingdoms, the kings of which are by no means arbitrary tyrants; they hold councils, or moots, of their subordinate chiefs, whose views they respect—and perhaps they respect even more the counsels of the court brāhmaṇs, who are very influential, especially the *purohita,* the chief priest. Also influential are the ascetics, living in the forests either in colonies or in lonely hermitages.

The early Pāli scriptures of Buddhism, perhaps referring to a period not long after the Buddha's death, agree with the *Mahābhārata* that the most important gods are Brahmā and Indra. Many other Vedic gods are still influential. None of the gods is omnipotent, but all can be overcome by determined ascetics through intense *tapas* (ascetic practices) and deep meditation. The ultimate neuter spirit, Brahman, which appears so frequently in the Upaniṣads, is hardly met with in the narrative of the epic and seems unknown to the Buddhists. On the other hand, both gods and men alike are constrained and controlled by impersonal forces such as the law of *karman* and a force often referred to as *daiva* or *vidhi*, which may be translated as fate. The concept of a power even higher than the gods is also found in Greek, Germanic, and other traditions of ancient Indo-European peoples.

The *Mahābhārata* gives glimpses of popular religion not evident in the Vedic literature, and these are confirmed and followed up by references to popular religion in the early scriptures of Buddhism, which seem to reflect conditions in an area of the Ganges valley rather to the east of that covered by the *Mahābhārata*. The most popular of the great gods are again Brahmā and Indra (known to the Buddhists as Sakka, or Śakra). Brahmā, apparently, was here generally recognized as the creator and guardian of the world, having taken over that function from the later Vedic Prajāpati. Indra ruled the lower heavens and was looked on as a rainmaker rather than as a war god.

The other gods of the Vedic pantheon still play important parts in the *Mahābhārata*, and Viṣṇu is rapidly gaining in importance and popularity, though Śiva has only a comparatively minor role. In the Buddhist literature the lesser Vedic gods play hardly any part at all. On the other hand here we meet many local nature spirits, known as *yakṣas*, and their female counterparts, the *yakṣīs*. In both Buddhist literature and the *Mahābhārata* these and epic demigods of another type are mentioned frequently. They are the *nāgas* and their wives, the *nāginīs*, strange magical serpents who dwell in a wonderful world of jewels and precious metal below the earth. They are conceived of as beautiful serpents, often with human heads, and they can, if they so choose, take on wholly human form. The worship of the *nāgas* probably emerged from the aboriginal inhabitants of the Ganges valley. These have been conventionally associated with almost any early religious innovation; but there is strong reason to believe that the cult of snakes had its beginning in non-Āryan circles, for the Vedic literature has nothing very good to say about them, and indeed Vṛtra, the arch-demon of chaos, is conceived of as a monstrous serpent. In classical mythology he was replaced by Śeṣa, the mighty seven-headed cobra on whose coils Viṣṇu sleeps during the cosmic night—a wholly benevolent divinity, representing endless time. *Nāgas*, according to both ancient and more recent belief, may be dangerous, but if treated with respect and won over with offerings of milk they might ring their patrons fortune and success. The real snake was also worshipped, and this is still done, mainly in the country districts, at a special festival in the rainy season.

The second of the great epics, the *Rāmāyaṇa*, is somewhat different in style from the *Mahābhārata*. Like so many early Indian texts, its chronology is much disputed. According to the orthodox tradition it describes events that took place about 870,000 years ago, and it was composed soon after that date. Thus it is fully qualified for the title given it as the *Ādikāvya*, the Primeval Poem. Modern Indians recognize that this fantastically early date is quite contrary to all the evidence of geology and prehistory, but they are still inclined to view the *Rāmāyaṇa* as older than the *Mahābhārata*. Rāma is the seventh *avatāra*, or incarnation, of Viṣṇu, while Kṛṣṇa is the eighth. Moreover, the *Mahābhārata* contains a brief version of the story of Rāma, while the *Rāmāyaṇa* betrays no knowledge of the story of the *Mahābhārata*. In considering these facts we must remember that the final list of ten *avatāras* is much later than either text; also we must make a clear distinction between the main narrative of the *Mahābhārata* and its interpolations, of which the story of Rāma is one. We have seen that there is clear evidence that the *Mahābhārata* was finally edited around 500 C.E. By that time the story of the *Rāmāyaṇa* was well known, as is shown by much other evidence. There are, in fact, weighty arguments in favour of the view that the *Rāmāyaṇa* is later than the narrative parts of the *Mahābhārata*. The *Rāmāyaṇa* seems to reflect a more developed political life than does the *Mahābhārata*. In the latter, kings and chiefs live in big halls, where they hold great assemblies of unruly nobles, with heavy drinking, gambling, and fierce quarrelling, sometimes ending in bloodshed. The court of Rāma's father, Daśaratha, at Ayodhyā is a much more developed institution, with a full corps of ministers and officials, chancellors and palace servants, courtiers and hangers-on—in fact, it is essentially little different from the court of a *mahārājan* in the early nineteenth century. Stylistically too, the *Rāmāyaṇa* seems much more sophisticated than the *Mahābhārata*. Much of the *Mahābhārata* narrative has a rugged, simple beauty but makes no pretences to high finish or intellectual style. The *Rāmāyaṇa*, on the other hand, seems the work of a conscious artist and looks forward to the rather ornate and cerebral style of classical Sanskrit literature. It is not a true martial epic in the sense of the *Mahābhārata*. If the *Mahābhārata* may be compared with the *Iliad*, the *Rāmāyaṇa* suggests Vergil's *Aeneid*, or in places even such florid Renaissance epics as Ariosto's *Orlando Furioso*.

The *Mahābhārata* is a text of many strata, but the *Rāmāyaṇa* is much less complex in structure. It consists of seven lengthy stages (*kāṇḍa*). The first book tells of the birth of Rāma, son of Daśaratha, king of Ayodhyā, and his brothers, Lakṣmaṇa, Bharata, and Śatrughna. Rāma goes to the court of King Janaka of

Videha (whom we have met before, in a more historically reliable context, as the patron of the sage Yājñavalkya) and wins the hand of his daughter Sītā in a contest in which he bends and breaks a mighty bow. The main story begins in the second book of the epic, when through the wiles of Daśaratha's second queen, Kaikeyī, Rāma is forced to go into exile with his faithful wife, Sītā, and his loyal brother Lakṣmaṇa. The trio settles as hermits in the Daṇḍaka forest in central India, and there the beautiful Sītā is kidnapped by the ten-headed demon king Rāvaṇa and is taken off to his palace in Laṅkā (Śrī Laṅkā). Her whereabouts are traced with the help of an army of monkeys, sent by Sugrīva, the monkey king of Kiṣkindha, and led by his general, Hanumat. Rāma and his monkey army build a causeway across the straits into Śrī Laṅkā and after a great battle Sītā is freed and the demon king and most of his army are slain. To prove that she has not yielded either to the threats or to the blandishments of the demon, Sītā undergoes an ordeal by fire, from which she emerges unscathed. Then the couple, with their retainers, return to Ayodhyā, where Rāma reigns long and righteously. This brings the sixth book to a close.

In the seventh book Rāma hears that his subjects resent the presence of Sītā in the royal palace because, despite her fire ordeal, her virtue is not beyond suspicion. Since his first duty is to please his subjects he feels compelled to send Sītā away, though he has no personal doubts as to her purity. She is exiled to the hermitage of the sage Vālmīki, the author of the *Rāmāyaṇa* according to tradition, where she gives birth to twin boys, Kuśa and Lava. Long afterward Rāma discovers them and wishes to take them with Sītā back to his palace. But Sītā gives a final proof of her purity by calling on her mother, the Earth, to take her back, for she was no ordinary woman but the daughter of the Earth Goddess herself, found as an infant by her putative father, Janaka, in the furrows of a ploughed field.[6] She stamps the earth, a chasm opens at her feet, and she disappears from sight.

There are many indications that the first and the seventh books are later additions. In the central story Rāma is, except in certain obvious interpolations, a mighty hero favoured by the gods; in the two later books he is the *avatāra* of the god Viṣṇu, as Kṛṣṇa is in the *Mahābhārata*—a special manifestation of the god whose mission is to save the cosmos from the attacks of demons. Moreover, the god Brahmā, who in the main body of the story seems to be the highest god of all, gives place in the first and seventh books to Viṣṇu, of whom Rāma is an incarnation.

The importance of the *Rāmāyana*, as far as popular religion is concerned, may be greater than that of the *Mahābhārata*. The story became very popular in later times, and adapted paraphrases of Vālmīki's epic were composed in all the languages of India, so that it became part of the folk literature of the land. It was carried to Southeast Asia and Indonesia, where it was equally popular. The story has had a strong ethical influence on the whole land. Rāma in the story is the epitome of all the virtues, an example to all people of honour, courage, and loyalty. In this respect he contrasts strikingly with the five Pāṇḍava brothers or Kṛṣṇa in the *Mahābhārata*, who for political ends occasionally stoop to deceit and trickery. Rāma always does the right thing. He cheerfully accepts exile so that his father may be true to his word; he never gives way to evil emotions such as rage and self-pity.[7] His brother Lakṣmaṇa is ethically almost his equal. Sītā is the ideal of wifely loyalty and faith, and her expostulation to Rāma, when he decides to go off to the forest without her, is one of the best-known passages of Sanskrit literature, laying down norms of womanly conduct that have exerted immense influence on Indian life down to the present day.

> So Rāma spoke, and Vaidehī [Sītā], who always spoke kindly to
> her husband and deserved kindness from him, grew angry
> just because she loved him, and said,

"My lord, a man's father, his mother, brother, son or daughter-in-law all experience the effects of their own past deeds and suffer an individual fate.

"But a wife, and she alone, bull among men, must share her husband's fate. Therefore I, too, have been ordered to live in the forest.

"It is not her father or mother, not her son or friends or herself, but her husband, and he alone, who gives a woman permanent refuge in this world and after death.

"If you must leave this very day for the trackless forest, Rāghava [Rāma], I will go in front of you, softening the thorns and sharp *kuśa* grass.

"Cast out your anger and resentment, like so much water left after drinking one's fill. Do not be reluctant to take me, my mighty husband. There is no evil in me.

"The shadow of a husband's feet in any circumstances surpasses the finest mansions, an aerial chariot, or even flying through the sky.[8]

"My mother and father instructed me in all the different questions. I do not have to be told now the proper way to behave.

"I shall live as happily in the forests as if it were my father's house, caring for nothing in the three worlds[9] but to be faithful to my husband.

"I will obey you always and practice self-discipline and chastity.[10] What pleasures I shall share with you, my mighty husband, in the honey-scented forests!

"O Rāma, bestower of honor, you have the power to protect any other person. Why then not me?

"You need not doubt that I can survive on nothing but fruit and roots; I shall not cause you any trouble by living with you.

"I want to see the streams and mountains, the ponds and forests, and nowhere shall I be afraid with my wise husband to defend me.

> "I want to see the lotus ponds in full bloom, blanketed with geese and ducks, happy in your company, my mighty husband.
>
> "What pleasures I shall share with you, my large-eyed husband, what bliss for me to be with you like this, were it for a hundred thousand years!
>
> "If I were to be offered a place to live in heaven itself, Rāghava, tiger among men, I would refuse it if you were not there.
>
> "I will go to the trackless forest teeming with deer, monkeys, and elephants, and live there as if in my father's house, clinging to your feet alone, in strict self-discipline.
>
> "I love no one else; my heart is so attached to you that were we to be parted I am resolved to die. Take me, oh please grant my request. I shall not be a burden to you."
>
> Despite what Sītā said, the best among men who so cherished righteousness, was still unwilling to take her, and in order to dissuade her, he began to describe how painful life in the forest is.[11]

The history of the divinization of Rāma is far from clear. The main story must have existed in a form much like its present one around the beginning of the common era. By the time of the Gupta dynasty (the fourth to sixth centuries C.E.) Rāma was evidently considered as an incarnation of Viṣṇu, theoretically on a par with Kṛṣṇa, but there is no evidence that at this time he was widely recognized. In fact the Rāma cult as an important feature of Indian religion appears to be quite late.

We might here mention one very important figure in the *Rāmāyaṇa,* that of Hanumat, the general sent by Sugrīva, the monkey king of Kiṣkindha. He is an essential figure in the story, for without his help Rāma would never have rescued Sītā. The monkeys of the *Rāmāyaṇa* are not ordinary monkeys, for they have the power of speech and their intelligence is equal to that of humans. In these earlier phases of the cycle of time the higher animals were all closer to humans and they could communicate with humans on equal terms.[12] Hanumat is a very special monkey, being the son of the wind god Vāyu, capable of tremendous feats of strength. He could make himself small or large at will, and in his later form he could travel immense distances simply by leaping through the air. He could make himself so enormous that he could carry a mountain on his back, or he could make himself so small that he could get through a mouse hole. Hanumat became a very popular god in his own right during the Middle Ages as a "very present help in trouble," especially in trouble of a practical or material kind. Just as he used his mighty strength to help Rāma, so he worked for the welfare of ordinary mortals. Believers had only to call Hanumat's name, with faith in their hearts, and he would do his utmost to help. The history of the cult of Hanumat is quite obscure, as there is no evidence for it before the beginning of the Gupta period. He seems to have begun in the Deccan as an obscure village deity, and his popularity appears to have spread with that of the *Rāmāyaṇa*.

SIX

The Bhagavad-Gītā *and the Triumph of Theism*

Included in the *Mahābhārata* is the *Bhagavad-gītā,* nowadays the most important and influential religious text of India. It is also the best-known Hindu text in the West, for it was the first to be translated into a European language (by the pioneer Sanskritist Charles Wilkins, in 1785), and versions of it exist in all the major languages of the world. It has been universally admired, a source of inspiration to millions of non-Hindus as well as to the descendants of those for whom it was originally composed.

The *Bhagavad-gītā* is, in a sense, the culmination of the ancient Upaniṣadic tradition. The name of the text does not mean, as it is usually loosely translated, "Song of the Lord" but "Sung by the Lord," with the participle in the feminine gender, modifying a feminine noun, namely *Upaniṣad*. Its full name, therefore, is *Bhagavad-gītopaniṣad,* "Upaniṣad Sung by the Lord." The work corresponds in many respects to the *Śvetāśvatara Upaniṣad,* which does for Śiva in briefer compass much the same as the *Bhagavad-gītā* does for Viṣṇu, making him the ultimate god, the source of the whole cosmos. But the *Bhagavad-gītā* contains elements that the *Śvetāśvatara* lacks and in its finished form is somewhat later.

Many readers of this book will have read the *Bhagavad-gītā* in one of its many translations, but for those who have not done so we must take note of the framework of the text, since this is most important for gaining an understanding of it and is often overlooked by scholars and students alike. The great battle of Kurukṣetra, which was to result in the triumph of the Pāṇḍavas and the annihilation of the Kauravas, is about to commence. On both sides mighty warriors are drawn up in battle array in their chariots. The air is loud with the strident sound of conchs blown by the troops on either side, each conch the treasured possession of its owner and given its own proper name. Suddenly Arjuna, the third of five Pāṇḍavas, has misgivings. He speaks to his friend Kṛṣṇa, who is acting as his charioteer. He is not so much afraid of being killed as of killing. His enemies are his kinsfolk, many of them known to him since childhood. They include elder statemen, wise counsellors, men of untarnished reputation and profound wisdom. Rather than kill such people, he would give up all his claims to the kingdom and become an ascetic. He does not wish to fight.

The chariot is stationed at a spot midway between the two armies, presumably to avoid the din of the conchs and the other sounds of battle, and there Kṛṣṇa presents a lengthy homily to Arjuna on the duty of the warrior and on many other topics. The whole consists of eighteen versified chapters of varying length. The verses too are of varying length, but the shortest and commonest is the *śloka* of thirty-two syllables. Excluding the first chapter, which contains the preliminary narrative and Arjuna's expression of his misgivings, the whole contains about 650 verses. A *śloka* takes at least twelve seconds to recite, which means that, even if Kṛṣṇa spoke without pause, he must have taken well over two hours to complete his sermon to Arjuna, even without the time taken by the wonderful theophany of the eleventh chapter. Yet the great battle was on the point of commencing.

This complete lack of proportion is not always noticed, since the *Bhagavad-gītā* is more often considered outside its context; but it is striking that, in the very moment before battle, Kṛṣṇa should have decided to give such a lengthy sermon, most of which has no direct relationship to Arjuna's moral quandary. In fact, his problem is settled with the thirty-eighth verse of the second chapter, after which Kṛṣṇa turns to other matters, many of which are irrelevant to the main theme. The answer is contained in less than one chapter and would take only a few minutes to recite. Scholars have tried to explain the incongruous length of the *Bhagavad-gītā* by appeals to the fact that Indian authors are said to lack a sense of proportion, to be illogical or inconsistent. Such generalizations are both unjust and inconclusive, and have little or no real weight. The most probable explanation is that the passage inserted into the *Mahābhārata* dealing with Arjuna's doubts and Kṛṣṇa's reassurance is the original text of the *Bhagavad-gītā* and the rest was added later.

Chapter one and chapter two down to verse 38 form a unity. They pose the ethical problem—is warfare justified?—and they answer it clearly and succinctly. Bodies can be killed, but you cannot kill the soul, which is eternal and must in any case pass from one body to another. Pleasure, pain, all the experiences of the senses are transitory and must be put up with—the wise man is the same in pleasure and pain, realizing that his soul is eternal and does not participate in the activities of everyday life. On gaining full awareness of the eternity of the soul he rises above mundane things and realizes that there is no cause for sorrow in death. Kṛṣṇa then adds a further, more practical argument: Arjuna is a member of the warrior class, and thus his class duty (*dharma*) is to fight in a just battle. If Arjuna does not do so he will become an object of scorn among friends and foes alike. On the other hand, if he is killed he will go straight to paradise. So he should gird himself for battle.

This brief, well-composed defence of righteous warfare, containing many memorable verses, was, we maintain, the original

Bhagavad-gītā. The rest was added later, by at least two hands. One of these was a philosopher of the Upaniṣadic type interested in the ultimate impersonal Brahman, which he considered the final truth of the universe. The other was an impassioned theist, a devotee of Viṣṇu especially in his incarnation as Kṛṣṇa Vāsudeva.

Evidence that, besides the brief "original" *Bhagavad-gītā*, there are at least two strata in the final text is provided by a later interpolation in the *Mahābhārata* known as the *Anugītā*, or Secondary Gītā, which occurs in the seventeenth book, the *Aśvamedha Parvan*, chapters sixteen to fifty-one. Here the war is long over and the Pāṇḍavas are at peace in their magnificent palace. Kṛṣṇa visits them. In conversation with him Arjuna reminds Kṛṣṇa of how he taught him on the battlefield and admits that he has forgotten Kṛṣṇa's words. Kṛṣṇa says, "It isn't possible for me to repeat in full what I said . . . when I declared the highest Brahman to you, but I'll tell you an old story on the same subject," after which follows a lengthy anthology of passages in the style of the verse Upaniṣads. There are many references to Brahman, to the three universal constituents (*guṇas*), to early forms of Sāṃkhya and Yoga philosophy in the *Anugītā*, but there is not one reference to the practice of devotion (*bhakti*) or to Kṛṣṇa's divinity. Yet the *Anugītā*, which is longer than the *Bhagavad-gītā* itself, purports to echo the doctrines of the latter. The most obvious conclusion is that the *Anugītā* was inserted into the *Mahābhārata* at a time when the *Bhagavad-gītā* was devoid of all its theistic passages.

This conclusion is strengthened by discrepancies and apparent contradictions in the text of the *Bhagavad-gītā* itself. Thus chapter five, verses 24 to 29, deals with the ultimate goal of the yogin, which is described as *Brahmanirvāṇa, Nirvāṇa* of Brahman. The sages who achieve this goal are those who delve deep within and control their breath and their senses. All taints and imperfections are destroyed in them, and their joy wells up from the Brahman within them. Such a sage is "truly liberated." Yet in the following and final verse (29) we read of such an advanced yogin, after he has attained *Brahmanirvāṇa:* "Then he learns to know me . . . the great lord of all the worlds, and then he reaches peace." It is surely impossible that this last verse is by the same hand that wrote the earlier ones. First we are told that the impersonal Brahman is the goal of the sage, the highest perfection, and then that it is a personal God in the form of Kṛṣṇa. Both propositions may be false, but they cannot both be true.[1] We submit that no one of sound mind could have composed verses 23 to 28 of the fifth chapter of the *Bhagavad-gītā* and then negated them as an afterthought with verse 29.

An analysis of the chapters of the *Bhagavad-gītā* shows that they fall into two main groups. The first of these consists of chapters two (verses 38 to the end), three, five, six, eight, thirteen, fourteen (verses 7 to 25), sixteen, seventeen, and eighteen (verses 1 to 53). Most of these chapters contain one or two verses in which Kṛṣṇa refers to himself as the highest god, but their main tenor is philosophical, explaining the nature of the cosmos and the highest state, referred to generally as Brahman. The theistic verses in these chapters are possibly the interpolations of a third author or compiler, who was responsible for chapters four, seven, nine, ten, eleven, fourteen (verses 1 to 6 and 26), fifteen, and seventeen (verses 54 to the end), which are passionately theistic.

The second stratum of the *Bhagavad-gītā* contains many very important passages that adumbrate some of the doctrines of later philosophical Hinduism. We are introduced to the doctrine of motiveless action: Whatever we do, we should do it because it is the right thing to do, without thought of personal gain or loss. This doctrine, developed out of the primary material, is the most important ethical teaching of the *Bhagavad-gītā*. Humans' business is with activity, work, and not with its results (2.47). Thought about the fruits of work, linked up with desire and selfhood, will prevent the integration of the self and the achievement of the highest spiritual goal. The doctrine that one should be selflessly active, one's only motive the fact that one's deeds were appropriate to the norms of one's class and stage of life (*varṇāśramadharma*), may have been evolved to reinforce the earlier arguments in favour of Arjuna's going into battle, but they may be adapted to every circumstance and any ethical code. Thus these passages inspired the pacifist Mahātmā Gāndhī, who did not believe in caste distinction and interpreted the battle of Kurukṣetra as taking place in the human soul, between good and evil impulses.

This second stratum also introduces several important concepts of later Hindu thought: the doctrine of the three *guṇas,* or universal constituents; the system of mental and spiritual training known as Yoga; the system of philosophy called Sāṃkhya, closely associated with Yoga; and the mystic impersonal absolute, Brahman. These are all mentioned in the Upaniṣads, but, with the exception of Brahman, they do not appear there in such detailed or developed form.

The word *guṇa* has as its first meaning thread, but in its philosophical sense it means constituent quality. The whole universe is permeated by the three *guṇas* in different proportions, which suggests that the term is applied on the analogy of three strands of a rope, twisted together. The three are *sattva* (virtue, goodness), *rajas* (passion, activity), and *tamas* (darkness, dullness). *Sattva* is associated with virtues and qualities such as wisdom, joy, altruism, and brightness; *rajas* with greed, ambition, activity, and anger; and *tamas* with idleness, ignorance, and delusion. The soul must strive to detach itself from all three *guṇas,* because even *sattva,* though it is pure and radiant, can serve as "the last infirmity of a noble mind," by causing the soul to cling to wisdom and joy (14.6). Everything in the universe is involved with the three *guṇas,* which form the basis of the qualities and values of life.

Yoga appears in the *Bhagavad-gītā* as a practical system of mental and spiritual development, whereby a man may reach complete detachment. When fully integrated the yogin views friends and enemies, good and evil, as the same (6.9). A little is said about the practice of yoga, which in this early period seems chiefly to have involved sitting completely still with body, neck, and head erect in a straight line and restraining thought and senses to make the mind a single point. To achieve this the yogin is advised to concentrate his eyes on the tip of his nose (6.11–13). The yoga of the *Bhagavad-gītā*, moreover, has a strong moral element and involves cultivating an attitude of calm benevolence (6.29, 32). Excluding a few theistic verses, which we believe are later additions, the goal of yoga is to become Brahman (6.27), the ultimate impersonal spirit.

Sāṃkhya in the *Bhagavad-gītā* is closely linked with Yoga, as the theoretical aspect of the yogic course of spiritual training. The clearest enunciation of the Sāṃkhya system in the *Bhagavad-gītā* is found in the thirteenth chapter, where a distinction is made between the field, or the material world, and the knower of the field, the soul. The field is defined as consisting of the five gross elements (earth, air, water, fire, and *ākāśa),*[2] the ego (*ahaṃkāra*), consciousness (*buddhi*), and the unmanifest (*avyakta*), which is equivalent to the Prakṛti (nature) of later Sāṃkhya, or the substratum of physical being, the first entity to emerge from Brahman. Together with these the field is composed of the eleven senses; on the basis of later Sāṃkhya classification these are the mind (the coordinating sense), the five senses of perception (hearing, touch, sight, taste, and smell), and the five senses of action (speech, grasping, locomotion, excretion, and copulation). The *Bhagavad-gītā* also adds certain emotions and sensations that do not occur in the later standard Sāṃkhya list—desire, aversion, pleasure, pain, thought, and constancy (13.1–6).

The categories enumerated in the field are contained in Prakṛti, generally translated as nature, and they evolved from Prakṛti one at a time in the process of creation. All phenomena take place in nature. Involved with nature is Puruṣa, literally "(male)

Person." Naturally quiescent, the Puruṣa becomes intimately linked with the three *guṇas* and the various components of Prakṛti. It is through the connection of Puruṣa and Prakṛti that the process of transmigration goes on (13.21), and the full and complete realization of the reality of Puruṣa and Prakṛti and the fundamental distinction between them leads to release from rebirth.

Behind all things is Brahman, the impersonal world spirit that forms one of the main themes of the Upaniṣads. Brahman is the goal of all spiritual striving. Brahman is realized by those who subdue all desires and who lose their sense of egoity. Such people draw near to Brahman in life, and on death they go to the *nirvāṇa* of Brahman (2.71–72). The term *nirvāṇa* as a definition of the highest state—where the specious personality disintegrates in a state of calm, indescribable bliss—is particularly associated with Buddhism, and the use of this word several times in the *Bhagavad-gītā* suggests that this philosophical stratum belongs to a period when Buddhism was well known.

This stratum of the *Bhagavad-gītā* also contains passages concerning sacrifice which are important and perhaps hark back to the passage in the *Chāndogya Upaniṣad* where all life is interpreted as a great sacrifice,[3] the doctrine learnt by Kṛṣṇa Devakīputra from the sage Ghora Āṅgirasa. In earlier Vedic contexts *karman* often meant religious activity, especially sacrifice. This same usage is continued in the *Bhagavad-gītā*. All human activity should be treated as a kind of sacrifice (4.23–33). Ritual sacrifices offered in a selfish spirit are sacrifices in name only (16.17). All ritual must be performed in self-surrender, without attachment to the result (18.6).

The third stratum of the *Bhagavad-gītā* is thoroughly theistic. It is the work of a literary genius, who infused the rather pedestrian verses of much of the second stratum with a new life, intense and moving. Rather than add his own verses to the end of the then existing text, he spread chapters and brief interpolations throughout the whole and gave it some degree of unity despite his doctrines being diametrically opposed to those of the earlier passages. It is not always easy to disentangle the second and third strata, but there appears at present no better method of explaining the evident discrepancies in the *Bhagavad-gītā*.

In this stratum the hero Kṛṣṇa, the friend and adviser of the Pāṇḍavas, becomes the incarnation of Viṣṇu, chief god and high god of the universe, from which all other entities, including Brahman, emanated. Ideas of a supreme personal divinity, also adumbrated in the *Śvetāśvatara Upaniṣad*, are here developed into positive doctrines spoken by God incarnate and therefore infallible. Once the framework of the *Bhagavad-gītā* is accepted it is evident that this is the word of God himself—not merely of a god. Thus the *Bhagavad-gītā* is worthy of as much respect as, or indeed even more than, the Vedas, and among several Vaiṣṇava sects of recent centuries the *Bhagavad-gītā* and certain other important Vaiṣṇava texts such as the *Bhāgavata Purāṇa* are referred to as the Vedas of the Dark, or Kali, Age.

Viṣṇu is God Almighty and contains all other gods as aspects of his being. All things and all beings have emanated from him and subsist in him (9.4).[4] This all-embracingness of the divine is particularly impressively brought out in the tremendous theophany, described in the eleventh chapter, where Kṛṣṇa displays himself to Arjuna in all the supernatural splendour of his transcendent form, with "the brilliance of a thousand suns." Evidently the theistic Vaiṣṇava cult had not long existed at the time of this part of the *Bhagavad-gītā* and was meeting some opposition: "The deluded world doesn't recognize me as unborn and changeless," says Kṛṣṇa (7.25). "Fools scorn me," he says elsewhere, "because I have taken on human form. They understand nothing of my higher nature as the Great Lord of all beings" (9.11).

As God, Kṛṣṇa underlies all thing, including the impersonal Brahman of the second stratum of the text. The theistic poet explains away the passages referring to Brahman by postulating this entity as subordinate to the personal God, and God as prior to Brahman. The harmonization of the new theistic passages with those emphasizing the ultimacy of Brahman, however, gave the final compiler some trouble, and discrepancies have not been completely eliminated. Thus in one place (3.30) the devotee is told by Kṛṣṇa, "Cast all your works on me"; yet a little later (5.10) he is told to put all his works on Brahman. Several passages clearly make Brahman inferior to Kṛṣṇa/Viṣṇu. Thus in a strange passage (14.3–4) Kṛṣṇa says, "My womb is the great Brahman, in that I place the embryo and thence is the arising of all beings. Those forms which arise and develop in every womb whatever, great Brahman is the womb of them, and I am their father, the giver of semen." Here the neuter Brahman seems to be equated with the feminine Prakṛti, the primeval nature, and becomes a sort of spouse of God, looking forward to the *śakti* of Tantrism.

The most important new doctrine in the *Bhagavad-gītā* is *bhakti,* devotion to God. This word is connected with the Sanskrit root *bhaj,* which has the sense of divide, participate, share. A person who feels the emotion of *bhakti* is a *bhakta,* a devotee, and God for the Vaiṣṇava is often referred to as *Bhagavan.* This word is generally translated as Lord and is also used by Buddhists with reference to the Buddha. The term may have originated with the feudal chieftains who shared the spoils of their successful campaigns with their followers. In any case the concept of *bhakti* has this deep undertone of participation in the divine, not merely the worshipping of a god at a great distance.

By *bhakti* the devotee may be assured of receiving God's grace. From the practical and material point of view *bhakti* is neither difficult nor expensive. It demands no costly sacrifices or severe penances, and God's grace can be obtained without the long course of yoga advocated in the second stratum of the text. A leaf, a flower, a fruit, a libation of water are sufficient offerings to God, provided they are given with loving devotion (9.26).

Bhakti offers, in fact, a shortcut to an advanced spiritual state that might be obtained by other methods only through great striving, penance, and pain. The attitude of *bhakti,* however, is not something that can be obtained merely by the recitation of suitable hymns and prayers, or by "vain repetitions." It involves constant consciousness and love of God. The doctrine of selfless, motiveless action in the earlier parts of the text is taken up in the later parts and given a theistic slant. Whatever a person does, he or she should do it for the love and glory of God, thinking of God always (9.27, 13.55–57).

The man who is perfected in *bhakti* is relieved of the burden of his past *karman.* This is one of the most important and striking of the corollaries of the new religious approach. Kṛṣṇa's grace can transcend all other factors, including the law of *karman.* This marks a very important stage in the evolution of Indian religious ideas. The doctrine of *karman,* as it was originally formulated, was a completely automatic system of reward and punishment. *Karman* was a law of nature, like the law of gravity, and it was believed that every bad deed had to be paid for in suffering. When it was first formulated, this doctrine seems to have been readily accepted; but the grim retributive justice of *karman* may have been found increasingly frightening, for in both Hinduism and Buddhism new religious forms evolved in which its sternness was mitigated. In Mahāyāna Buddhism the heavenly Buddhas and Bodhisattvas, with their great spiritual power and merit, could set aside *karman.* In Hinduism, similarly, the grace of God, the author of the law of *karman,* could abrogate its punishments. Thus in the *Bhagavad-gītā* we are told that even if a man of very evil conduct devotes himself to Kṛṣṇa alone, his pious intention will count as virtue, his soul will quickly become righteous, and he will go to eternal rest. Even *śūdras* and women, who have no right to hear the Vedas or to perform the rituals of the brāhmaṇs, will reach the highest goal if they develop an attitude of *bhakti* toward God (9.30–32). The text lays much emphasis, as do some Upaniṣads, on the last state of mind of a dying person as promoting salvation. In one place, indeed, Kṛṣṇa declares that the man who at the hour of death bears him in mind with devotion goes straight to him (8.5). Thus it behoves a man to bear God in mind at all times, especially if he is at war, when his life is in danger (8.7).

Kṛṣṇa does not reject the reality of other gods, but they are all subsumed in him and emanate from him. Thus those who worship and sacrifice to other gods with devotion and faith are in fact worshipping Kṛṣṇa, though they do not know him as he really is (9.23–24). This is typical of the general inclusive attitude of later Hinduism, where every minor god everywhere has some validity, as an aspect of the one divinity filling all space and time.

One of the most important new doctrines of the *Bhagavad-gītā* is that of *avatāra,* "coming down," that is, incarnation. Kṛṣṇa appears to be a normal human being who has been reborn many times in the normal way (4.5). Yet he is also the unborn Lord of all beings, who through his supernatural power (*māyā*)[5] has come to be in human form (4.6). The process is not made very clear, and here we are at the very beginning of the doctrine of *avatāras,* when its theology had not been fully worked out. It appears from verses 5 and 6 of chapter four that, for the protection of the good, the destruction of the evil, and the establishment of righteousness (4.8), the Supreme Person, Viṣṇu, decided to project himself into the yet unborn son of Vāsudeva and came into being as Kṛṣṇa, who also had a normal history of earlier rebirths. Thus he was not a wholly supernatural being but, as in Christian theology, was both man and god simultaneously.

From the point of view of the *Bhagavad-gītā,* Kṛṣṇa is not the only *avatāra.* "Whenever righteousness (*dharma*) fails and unrighteousness raises its head," says Kṛṣṇa, "I come to birth on earth." But no other *avatāras* are mentioned by name. Much later a standard list of ten *avatāras* became current, including Rāma, the hero of the *Rāmāyaṇa,* but there is no sign of such a list here. On the other hand there are, in a sense, a number of partial incarnations of Kṛṣṇa, for "I am the reason in the rational, the glory in the glorious, the power devoid of passion and desire in the powerful" (7.10–11), and "whatever is powerful, fortunate or strong springs from a portion of my glory" (10.41). Indeed the theology of the theistic portions of the *Bhagavad-gītā* has much in common with that of Christianity, and this may be one of the reasons it has been so widely read in the Western world.

A feature of the *Bhagavad-gītā* which has aroused criticism in modern times is its sturdy defence of the system of the four classes. "It is better," says Kṛṣṇa, "to perform one's own duty, however badly, than to do another's well. It is better to die engaged in one's own duty; the duty of other men is dangerous" (3.35). The word for duty here is *dharma,* and the poet has in mind the respective *dharmas* of the four classes. This verse is repeated with variations elsewhere in the *Bhagavad-gītā* (e.g., 18.47) and in the *Dharma Śāstra* literature of a somewhat later time. Modern interpreters of the *Bhagavad-gītā* are inclined to ignore or reinterpret the passages dealing with the class system, but it is quite clear that the text is a defence not only of the warrior's duty to wage righteous warfare but also of the whole brāhmaṇic social system. This also suggests a date a century or two before the common era, when Buddhists and others were strongly criticizing the doctrine of the four classes and declaring that birth made no difference to a person's fundamental merit and value.

The first half of the eighteenth and last chapter of the *Bhagavad-gītā* sums up the teaching of the text on class very explicitly, within the framework of a doctrine of desireless action. Brāhmaṇs, warriors, middle-class folks (*vaiśyas*), and the lower classes (*śūdras*) have their own specific tasks, duties that depend on the classes' composition in respect of the three *guṇas*. Humans should gladly do the work appropriate to them, dedicating all work to God, working as best they can at their vocations, because this is the appropriate thing to do. Thus people can train themselves in detachment and ultimately reach Brahman.

Our interpretation of the *Bhagavad-gītā* is rather unorthodox and may be controverted by an important school of exegetes who follow the interpretation of the great schoolman of early mediaeval Hinduism, Śaṅkarācārya, who lived from about the end of the eighth to the beginning of the ninth century C.E. To his own satisfaction, Śaṅkarācārya explained away the theistic elements and interpreted the text as a thoroughly monistic document. Interpretations of this kind are of no more value in showing us what the compilers of the *Bhagavad-gītā* really had in mind in writing as they did than are the fantastic though very clever interpretations of certain parts of the Hebrew Bible by mediaeval schoolmen. Such scholars, often brilliant intellectually, already knew the meaning of such texts as the Song of Songs and set to work to iron out apparent discrepancies and inconsistencies, without the least attempt to understand the minds of the ancient Jewish poets who composed the texts. We need not disparage either the mediaeval commentators on Hinduism or the schoolmen of mediaeval Christianity: They produced brilliant philosophical systems and did much to promote the religious systems in which they believed; their aims, however, were completely different from those of modern critical scholarship, which as far as possible approaches such texts with an open mind. Ancient texts must be allowed to speak for themselves, and on this basis the *Bhagavad-gītā* emerges as a compilation by more than one hand, with at least two main authors whose doctrines are very different.

The chronology of the text presents great problems and cannot be established except very vaguely. The first part of the

Bhagavad-gītā suggests that it was composed at a time when the ethics of the warrior, glorifying righteous warfare and stressing the martial virtues, were being questioned. This indicates that the whole of the *Bhagavad-gītā* is posterior to the rise of Buddhism and Jainism in the fifth century B.C.E. and especially the time of the peace-loving Buddhist emperor Aśoka in the third century B.C.E. It is possible that the earliest part of the text was composed before the doctrine of transmigration was fully accepted and understood because certain verses (especially 2.13, 22, and 27) seem to be composed for the benefit of listeners who do not completely understand it. In the second phase of the text (16.8), according to our stratification, we find another verse that may be directed against Buddhists.

> "The world has no virtue," they [the anxious persons] say,
> "No basis, no Lord,
> It has not come about through causation.
> It is caused by desire only."

This suggests not the early Buddhists, but the Mahāyānists with their doctrine of vacancy (*śunyatā*), which may have begun in the early centuries B.C.E. though the texts describing it are later.

We can find some evidence for the date of the final theistic stratum. The existence of a sect of worshippers of a god whose favourite name was Vāsudeva (meaning son of Vasudeva) but who was also known as Kṛṣṇa is evident from inscriptions and other sources from the second century B.C.E. onward. These people often called themselves Bhāgavatas, worshippers of the *Bhagavan,* the Lord, a term that was speedily appropriated by the followers of Viṣṇu and his incarnations. Coins of a Greek king, Antialcidas, ruling from the great northwestern city of Taxila (Takṣaśilā, not far from modern Islāmabād, Pakistān), bear figures that have been identified as Kṛṣṇa and his brother Bālarāma, who was also looked on as a divinity. Heliodorus, an envoy of the same Antialcidas of Taxila, erected a fine pillar at

Besnagar, the headquarters of the Śuṅga kings near Vidiśāpur (Bhīlsā) in Madhya Pradesh. Again the date cannot be established precisely, but Antialcidas must have been reigning around 100 B.C.E. Several other brief inscriptions of about the same time show that by now the Bhāgavata cult was firmly established. Thus we can suggest that the *Bhagavad-gītā* was complete in its final form not much later than about 100 B.C.E. and that its compilation may have covered two hundred years or more.

SEVEN

The Ritual and Dharma *Literature and the New Hindu Orthodoxy*

In this chapter we complete the discussion of classical Hinduism by expanding several of the topics previously introduced. We shall then briefly trace the developments in Hinduism to the present day, paying particular attention to those forms found in the West.

An important class of *smṛti,* remembered literature, known as the *Kalpa Sūtras,* or Manuals of (Vedic) Ritual, was mentioned only briefly in preceding chapters. These are short texts ascribed to particular sages, dating from around the sixth century B.C.E. Being attached to a particular Vedic school, they belong to the larger corpus of Vedāṅgas, or Appendages to the Veda. Focussing on ritual, ethics, and law, they form the backbone of early Hinduism. They are divided into three groups, *Śrauta, Gṛhya,* and *Dharma Sūtras,* and derive for the most part from the earlier ritualistic Vedic literature of the Brāhmaṇas.

These new treatises were composed in the style of short aphoristic phrases or sentences, known as *sūtras,* threads. Their purpose was to offer a concise presentation of a particular religious system so that a student could easily commit it to memory; the ideal *sūtra* was one that said much in few words. As fabric consists of many threads woven together, so also the different

religious systems of the Veda are made up of the prose *sūtras*. When the *sūtra* was memorized, a properly qualified priestly teacher then provided its full elucidation.[1] These elaborate explanations were essential for the correct understanding of the *sūtras* and eventually were written down as commentaries on the original text.

With the passage of time, the ritual instructions of the Brāhmaṇas became too complex and obscure, so that a new set of texts was required to elucidate the sacrificial procedures and to preserve the traditional practices. The books composed to bring about this end were the *Śrauta Sūtras,* Manuals Explaining the Revealed Scriptures (*śruti*). They gave instructions for the establishment of the three sacred fires of the fire sacrifice (*agnihotra*) as well as for other Vedic rituals. Directly connected to the *Śrauta Sūtras* are the *Śulva Sūtras,* which are exact rules for the measurement and the construction of the sacred sacrificial ground and of the fire altars. They are the oldest works on Indian geometry and religious architecture.

Following the *Śrauta Sūtras,* the *Gṛhya Sūtras,* Manuals Explaining the Domestic (*gṛhya*) Religious Ceremonies, were composed. Along with descriptions of many popular customs, these texts contain ritual procedures for the performance of the *saṃskāras,* or Hindu sacraments, some forty in number, which cover the entire life of a person from the time of conception to the hour of death and include funeral ceremonies and rites devoted to the departed soul (*śrāddha*). The most important ones—centring around conception and the child, initiation as a twice-born (*dvija*), education, marriage, and death—are still performed by pious Hindus. The *Gṛhya Sūtras* contain many interesting parallels to manners and customs, especially surrounding marriage, common to the wider group of Indo-European peoples.

The third group of the *Kalpa Sūtras* is made up of the *Dharma Sūtras,* Manuals Explaining (Proper) Human Conduct (*dharma*). Dating from about the seventh to the second centuries

B.C.E., they were one of the most significant developments of early Hinduism, for they established the norms for the social and ritual behaviour of every Hindu and laid down the basis of civil law. They were composed by brāhmaṇs—priests and savants of a particular Vedic school—especially for the purpose of giving instructions to the adherents of that school. They were not meant as codes for use in courts of law but were considered to have absolute authority in secular and religious matters pertaining to the duties and rites of brāhmaṇs.

These *dharma* treatises cover a wide range of subjects, encompassing religious matters—including rules for the devotion to gods, for purification and expiatory rites, and for the use of food—as well as lectures on cosmology, cosmogony, and eschatology and sections on civil, criminal, and family law. Most importantly, they established the rules for the proper behaviour of members of the Āryan community. For the first time, they set down the precise ordinances pertaining to the four stations of life (*āśramas*), which applied to every male member of the three higher Hindu classes. After being invested with the sacred thread, the newly initiated twice-born boy shed his childhood and became a *brahmacārin,* leading a celibate and austere life as a student in the house of his teacher (*guru*). After having mastered the Vedas and other pertinent *smṛti* literature, the young man returned home, wed, and settled down to a productive life as a householder (*gṛhastha*). When he had raised his family, secured the marriage of his children, and established his line of descent, the man, nearing his twilight years, retired to the forest to become a hermit (*vānaprastha*) and to seek deeper spiritual wisdom. Engaging in meditation and austerities, he, as an old man, finally left the security of the hermitage to become a wandering mendicant (*sannyāsin*), relinquishing the bonds to his previous existence and devoting himself to the final goal of release (*mukti*) from the endless cycle of birth, death, and rebirth.

The three *Kalpa Sūtras* are ascribed to certain legendary sages. The same author is thought to have composed a text in each of the three categories, although the only surviving examples of such are those by Baudhāyana and Āpastamba. Thus the sage Baudhāyana was the author of manuals on *śrauta, gṛhya,* and *dharma.* The most important *Dharma Sūtras* are ascribed to Gautama, Baudhāyana, and Vasiṣṭha, along with Āpastamba.

During the early centuries of the common era, the prose *sūtras* were expanded, remodelled in verse, and called the *Dharma Śāstras,* Instructions in Sacred Law. Unlike the circumscribed *Dharma Sūtras,* these larger *dharma* textbooks were meant as instructions in religious and secular duties for all members of the Āryan community and, as such, were used in courts of law. Although pertaining to all Āryans, they devote considerable attention to the rights and duties of the king, who, by this time, was considered to be a god among humans. Their express purpose, however, was more religious than secular (although in India, the two are often hardly separable): They provided instruction in the way to salvation.

Numerous *Dharma Śāstras* were composed, the earliest of which was the *Mānava Dharma Śāstra* or the *Manu Smṛti,* usually called the Laws of Manu, dating from around the second century B.C.E. to the first century C.E. Being a collection of ancient and irrefutably valid precepts, Manu's was far and away the most important of the textbooks on *dharma.* Others, however, included the law books of Yājñavalkya, Viṣṇu, and Nārada, which date from the early centuries C.E. In the mediaeval period (eighth to twelfth centuries), *dharma* texts were composed in great numbers, all claiming to have the authority of the ancient treatises.

Although the *Dharma Śāstras* offered only a model of a perfectly ordered society, they provided the basis of cohesion that helped to unite the orthodox brāhmaṇic tradition in the face of the growing threat from the heterodox ascetic movements of Buddhism, Jainism, and Ājīvikism, among others.

Dharma, the religious and social duty of a good Hindu, is the common thread running through Hinduism. The origins of *dharma* lie in the Ṛg-vedic concept of *ṛta,* the course of things or the cosmic order, the maintenance of which was entrusted to the god Varuṇa (see chapter 1). Derived from the Sanskrit root *dhṛ*—to bear, to support, to maintain—the word *dharma* has the literal meaning of that which is established, that is, law, duty, or custom. The concept pertained to everything that was right and proper for a member of the Āryan community.

The exemplary treatise on *dharma* is the *Manu Smṛti,* considered such an important source of Hindu law and custom throughout the whole of the subcontinent that it was one of the earliest texts earmarked by the British for translation to be used in British courts in India. In 1794, the English rendering by Sir William Jones was published posthumously under the title *Institutes of Hindoo Law.*

This textbook of Hindu law and custom devotes over three-fourths of its precepts to religious instruction; about one-fourth concerns matters of civil law. Most importantly, it details the principles of the *varṇāśramadharma,* the duties (*dharma*) in accordance with class (*varṇa*) and stage of life (*āśrama*), only adumbrated in the earlier prose works of *Dharma Sūtras.* The fundamental notions of class and stages of life have been previously discussed; their full elaboration is found, however, for the first time in this, the earliest of the *Dharma Śāstras.*

The *Manu Smṛti* has a close connection to the epic text of the *Mahābhārata,* which contains several direct quotations from *Manu,* and numerous of its instructions are similar to those found in the law book. The subsequent textbooks on *dharma* are for the most part modelled on *Manu* and modify, supplement, or expand what was already established in it, based on rethinking in light of current trends, regional diversities, and social pressures. A notable exception is the *Yājñavalkya Smṛti,* which stands next to *Manu* in both age and authority, dating from around the first to second century C.E. Its teachings are generally more modern and more advanced. Likewise, its material is more concise, clearer, and more systematically presented, treating in three sections of approximately equal length customs (*ācāra*), judicial procedures (*vyavahāra*), and expiations (*prāyaścitta*).

Practically every aspect of the ideal life of Hindu men and women is addressed in the *Dharma Śāstras,* leaving no doubt as to the proper course of conduct in a given situation. Having mastered the Veda, the twice-born turned his attention to the study of the *dharma* texts until they also were part of his storehouse of knowledge. These didactic treatises were in the sole domain of the learned brāhmaṇs, who established and changed the precepts as the need arose and whose consultation was required in all matters pertaining to *dharma.* The *Dharma Śāstras* were used in legal actions involving cases of one class member against another and infringements of the sacred law by individual class members and in civil matters involving all levels of society.

Generally, the laws tended to favour men of the higher orders, the brāhmaṇ being less severely punished for infractions against his underlings. Thus, for example, according to Basham, "A brāhmaṇ slandering a kṣatriya should, according to Manu, pay a fine of fifty paṇas,[2] but for slandering a vaiśya or a śūdra the fines are only twenty-five and twelve paṇas respectively. For members of the lower orders who slander their betters the penalties are more severe. Similar gradations of penalty according to the class of the offender are laid down for many crimes, and the equality of all before the law was never admitted in ancient India."[3] There were, however, exceptions to this general trend. According to *Manu,* in crimes of theft, the gradation of the fine was lowest for the *śūdra* and highest for the brāhmaṇ. Perhaps realizing that the inequalities manifest in a stratified society were bound to breed contempt, certain compassionate lawmakers included laws tending to favour those who wanted, rather that those who had all they needed. Nevertheless, as Basham points out, "The upper classes were expected to follow higher standards of conduct than the lower, and their thefts were correspondingly more heinous."[4]

The woman's status in ancient India was always inferior to that of the man, her punishment for wrongdoing being, according to the law books, equivalent to that given a *śūdra*. The law, however, allowed her to own a modest amount of personal property (*strīdhana*) in the form of jewellery and clothing, which, in times of difficulty, could be sold by her husband. But when she died her property went to her female offspring rather than to her husband or sons.

Although there are literary references to religiously inclined women, a female's principal role was as a dutiful wife and a caring mother. We have already seen the image of Sītā as the ideal wife portrayed in the beautiful passage from the *Rāmāyaṇa*. The law book of Manu clearly defines the wife's duties.

> She should do nothing independently
> even in her own house.
> In childhood subject to her father,
> in youth to her husband,
> and when her husband is dead to her sons,
> she should never enjoy independence. . . .
>
> She should always be cheerful,
> and skilful in her domestic duties,
> with her household vessels well cleansed,
> and her hand tight on the purse-strings. . . .
>
> In season and out of season
> her lord, who wed her with sacred rites,
> ever gives happiness to his wife,
> both here and in the other world.

Though he be uncouth and prone to pleasure,
    though he have no good points at all,
the virtuous wife should ever
    worship her lord as god.[5]

Women of upper classes were generally kept at a distance from the opposite sex, and the husband in principle controlled his wife's every movement. With the coming of the Muslims in the tenth century, Hindus in northern India adopted the system of *parda,* whereby women from puberty to old age were screened from the sight of all men save their husbands and close relatives. Influences from the Tamils in the south during the eighth to the twelfth centuries, however, gave women new importance in some Hindu religious circles (see the discussion of Śāktism later in the chapter), leading to the loosening of many restrictions placed on females by male-dominated Hindu society. The observance of *parda* began to be abandoned. Today it is almost completely ignored by Hindu women. Women in India currently enjoy a greater amount of freedom and opportunity than they had in the past, owing to the reform movements of the past century.[6]

This short summary of the *Kalpa Sūtras* and the *Dharma Śāstras* is designed to tie together the references to these subjects in earlier chapters. The notion of *dharma* surfaces time and again in Hindu literature. It is a central theme in the original *Bhagavad-gītā.* To maintain his upright standing in the warrior class, Arjuna must engage in a just battle. Scholars have argued that this plea that a warrior perform his class duty was a way of stating that all four classes should faithfully adhere to their respective class duties. The mere mention of it in this context, therefore, indicates that the principle of *varṇāśramadharma* was beginning to lose its strong grip on the Āryan community in the face of the growing popularity of the antibrāhmaṇic heterodox religious movements.

Representing the pinnacle of the development of classical Hinduism, the *Bhagavad-gītā,* through successive interpolations by Hindu theologians, was able to arrest the decay of the orthodox socioreligious tradition and to pave the way for the rejuvenation of the brāhmaṇic religion that was to follow. To do so, however, a reshaping of the earlier notions of the absolute, the sacrifice, and one's class duty had to take place. This transformation marks the beginning of the new form of Hinduism, characterized by, among other things, theism and devotion to a supreme deity, a personification of the abstract Upaniṣadic Brahman. This trend appears in the latter two strata of the *Bhagavad-gītā* and was developed by Hindu theologians in successive centuries.

The Hinduism of the first millennium of the common era saw developments already indicated in the epics and, in particular, in the *Bhagavad-gītā.* The Smārtas, those who followed the teachings of the *smṛtis,* maintained the orthodox brāhmaṇic doctrine of *varṇāśramadharma.* The new trend toward theism, however, was becoming a dominant force in Hinduism with the growth of sectarianism, centring on the divinities Viṣṇu, Śiva, and Śakti, the feminine emanation of Śiva. At the same time, a new form of worship of a deity (*pūjā*), usually in a temple, was replacing the old form of Vedic sacrifice (*yajña*).

We find the most important record of the theistic movements in the later literary forms known as the Purāṇas, Ancient Stories, which are compendia of religious, secular, and mythical information traditionally focussing on five topics: the creation of the cosmos, the re-creation of the cosmos after its periodic destruction and reabsorption, the genealogies of gods and sages, the ages of the world and their rulers, and the genealogies of great kings. *Dharma* teachings are included alongside stories of the principal gods Viṣṇu and Śiva, and there are obvious attempts to appeal to women and *śūdras.*

Most authorities posit eighteen chief Purāṇas, the most important of which are the *Vāyu, Viṣṇu, Agni, Bhaviṣya,* and *Bhā-*

gavata Purāṇas. Titles of others bear the names of different *avatāras* of the god Viṣṇu, including *Kūrma,* Tortoise, *Vārāha,* Boar, *Matsya,* Fish, and *Vāmana,* Dwarf. The extant forms of the Purāṇas are relatively recent, dating not much before the Gupta period (the fourth to sixth centuries C.E.), but much of their legendary material is quite ancient.

The *Vāyu Purāṇa* describes best the Śaivas, or sects devoted to the worship of Śiva. The *Viṣṇu Purāṇa,* the *Harivaṃśa*—an appendix to the *Mahābhārata* traditionally considered to be a Purāṇa—and the later *Bhāgavata Purāṇa* best represent the beliefs and practices of Vaiṣṇavas, the devotees of Viṣṇu.

The *Vāyu Purāṇa* presents the followers of Śiva as naked, ash-covered ascetics with matted hair, begging for food, reclining in dirt, and living in cemeteries. Contrary to brāhmaṇic orthodoxy, women and *śūdras* were openly admitted to the sects, whose principal symbol was the *liṅgam,* or erect penis, which represented Śiva's power obtained by the ascetic practice of withholding and storing up semen.

The *Viṣṇu Purāṇa* and the *Harivaṃśa* continue the Vaiṣṇava doctrines begun in the *Bhagavad-gītā* but add a very important element in the story of Kṛṣṇa not found in the earlier epics: Kṛṣṇa's youth as a cowherd, or Kṛṣṇa Gopāla. This legend, derived from contacts with the cowherd tribes of Ābhīras, who lived in north-central and western India, tells about Kṛṣṇa as a young boy. Central to Kṛṣṇa's childhood is his dance with the milkmaids (*gopīs*), called the *rāsa-līlā,* which eventually became the object of worship by many of the devotional sects. This episode describes Kṛṣṇa's intense love for the *gopīs* and their love of him long after his departure from them. It illustrates that the human emotion of love was but a form of devotion to God. When intense love, such as that which the *gopīs* had for Kṛṣṇa, was directed toward the Lord, the devotee was performing *bhakti,* a form of religious practice advocated in the *Bhagavad-gītā* and fully elaborated in the *Bhāgavata Purāṇa*. Salvation by means of devotion was now open to all humans regardless of birth, gender, or station in life. The movement grew rapidly, giving, for the first time, women and the lower social orders equal access to salvation.

The rise of Hindu theism and sectarianism during the Gupta period led to the construction of permanent stone structures, or temples, to house the great images of the deities which were being produced. Along with these, there emerged a new way of propitiating the divinities, known as *pūjā*.

The political leaders of the Gupta dynasties were followers of Hinduism and the boar (*varāha*) incarnation of Viṣṇu became their symbol of royal power. Theism was the state religion. Under royal patronage, temples were constructed and became the principal repositories of wealth and religious art. Textbooks on temple design (*Śilpa Śāstras*) were composed, detailing every aspect of a structure that was considered symbolic of the cosmos. Great Hindu temples from this period onward can still be found throughout the subcontinent of India.

The temples were and are the principal centres for the worship of a deity by means of *pūjā,* which, according to Basham, "is not so much an act of prayer as of homage and entertainment."[7] Important temples had a large staff of trained officiants who attended to the divinity. At a typical *pūjā* in a temple, "The god is offered water for washing the feet, flowers and betel quids, like an honoured guest. In the morning he is ceremonially awakened with the sound of music, the ringing of bells, and the blowing of conches. He is washed, dried and dressed. He is honoured with flowers, garlands, incense and swinging lamps; he is fed, usually rice and fruit, of which he eats the subtle part, leaving the gross material food for his worshippers, or to be given to the poor. . . . he is taken to his bedroom at night where he joins his wife or wives. In large shrines he is fanned by attendants and entertained by dancing girls [*devadāsīs*] like any ancient Indian king."[8] A much simpler form of *pūjā* would be performed before images in the home.

30. Śiva Bhairava (*Pahārī* [*North India*], *nineteenth century; collector: Charles Craig.*) This composite picture of the terrible aspect of Śiva depicts his decapitation of Brahmā's fifth head and his penance to live as a beggar for committing such an evil.

31. Varāha (boar incarnation of Viṣṇu). (*Location unknown, ninth–tenth century; collector: Charles Craig.*) This image depicts the third avatāra (incarnation) of Viṣṇu on whose left arm sits the earth goddess (Bhūdevī).

32. Śiva holding the serpent. (*Location unknown, twelfth century; collector: Charles Craig.*) This representation of the god is a variation of Śiva as accompanied with a skeleton (*kaṅkāla-mūrti*) in which he is depicted as holding a serpent.

33. Durgā seated on a lion. (*Location unknown, tenth century; collector: Charles Craig.*) In this example of Hindu Śāktism, the goddess Durgā, a personification of the female power of Śiva, is depicted as seated on her vehicle, the lion.

34. ŚRĪ NĀTHAJĪ (Kṛṣṇa as Cosmic Lord). (*Nāthdwāra, Rājasthān [North India], nineteenth century; collector: Charles Craig.*) In this scene from a fifteenth-century Vaiṣṇava addition to the Kṛṣṇa story, the Lord holds up Mount Govardhana to protect the inhabitants from torrential rains unleashed by the jealous god Indra.

35. VIṢṆU. (*Nāthdwāra, Rājasthān [North India], nineteenth century; collector: Charles Craig.*) In this scene Viṣṇu is shown in the wish-granting gesture, surrounded by attendants performing *pūjā* to the god.

36. Śɪᴠᴀ, Pāʀᴠᴀᴛī, Sᴋᴀɴᴅᴀ, ᴀɴᴅ Gᴀṇᴇśᴀ. (*Pahārī [North India], [?], nineteenth century; collector: Charles Craig.*) This scene depicts Śiva with his family: his wife, Pārvatī, and their children Skanda or Kārttikeya and Gaṇeśa.

37. Vɪṣṇᴜ. (*Location unknown, ninth–tenth century; collector: Charles Craig.*) Viṣṇu in the standing position represents perhaps Nārāyaṇa, the Universal Abode. He is surrounded by flying attendants and three seated deities, representing perhaps the Hindu Trinity (Brahmā, Viṣṇu, and Śiva).

38. Śɪᴠᴀ ᴀɴᴅ Pᴀ̄ʀᴠᴀᴛɪ̄. (*Pahārī [North India], nineteenth century; collector: Charles Craig.*) In this scene, the ash-covered ascetic Śiva is shown with his wife Pārvatī.

39. Fᴇᴍᴀʟᴇ ᴀᴛᴛᴇɴᴅᴀɴᴛ. (*Location unknown, eleventh century; collector: Charles Craig.*) This unidentified female attendant is shown holding a fly whisk in her left hand and the sun disc on a lotus in her right hand.

40. Kailāsanātha cave temple. (*Ellorā [South India], eighth century; collector: James A. Santucci.*) This is a fine example of a South Indian Śaiva cave-type temple. Its name derives from Śiva's mountain throne atop Mount Kailāsa in North India.

41. Indra. (*Ellorā [South India], ninth–tenth century; collector: James A. Santucci.*) This image of Indra is found in the Jaina cave, known as Indra Sabhā, and depicts the Vedic war god mounted on his vehicle, the elephant Airāvata, and flanked by two attendants.

42. Viśvakarman cave temple. (*Ellorā [South India], ninth–tenth century; collector: James A. Santucci.*) The temple (*caitya*) is dedicated to the god Viśvakarman, the architect of the gods and current patron of artisans. The picture shows the ornately decorated entrance to the cave temple.

43. Ambikā. (*Ellorā [South India], ninth–tenth century; collector: James A. Santucci.*) Situated facing Indra in the Jaina cave (See illus. 41), Ambikā is the female messenger of the twenty-second Jaina saint Nemi and wife of Nemi's attendant Gomedha. She is depicted as seated on a lion.

44. Hanumat. (*South India, nineteenth century; collector: Ingrid Aall.*) The monkey god Hanumat, ally of Rāma, serves as the handle of a temple bell.

45. Buddha. (*Laos, nineteenth century; collector: Ingrid Aall.*) In this position, the Buddha is depicted as "touching the earth," representing the Buddha's defeat of the demon Māra immediately before his enlightenment.

46. Garuḍa (*Laos, eighteenth–nineteenth century; collector: Ingrid Aall.*) The vehicle of Viṣṇu, Garuḍa is shown as half bird and half human.

47. Kālī. (*Bengal, twentieth century; collector: Ingrid Aall.*) The multi-armed goddess Kālī with tongue out, wearing a garland of skulls and holding a severed head in one hand, represents the terrible, destructive power of Śiva.

On festive days, the deity would be removed from his temple home and paraded in the streets on an ornate palanquin (*ratha*, or chariot). The most famous of these religious celebrations is the annual procession of Viṣṇu as Jagannātha, Lord of the World, which takes place at Purī in Orissā. In the past, people would accidentally or as a sacrificial act be crushed under the massive wheels of Viṣṇu's *ratha*. (From this we get the word *juggernaut*.)

In Śaiva circles, *pūjā* is performed before the symbolic representations, or icons (*arcā*), of Śiva's dual nature. The *liṅgam*, or phallus, symbolizes his male power and the *yoni*, or womb, his female creative power, or *śakti*. Both are present in the one deity, who is often iconographically depicted as half male and half female (*ardhanārīśvara*).

Temple worship and *pūjā* characterize Hindu religious practice to the present day, and many great temples of India remain very wealthy institutions.

The Smārta tradition derived from the Purāṇic tradition, which combined the principles of *varṇāśramadharma* with *pūjā* to popular gods. Rather than reverencing a single supreme deity however, Smārtas worshipped five divinities: Viṣṇu, Śiva, Sūrya (the Vedic sun god), Gaṇeśa (the elephant-headed deity, son of Śiva and Pārvatī), and Durgā (Śiva's consort). Moreover, unlike sectarian rituals of the Śaivas and Vaiṣṇavas, Smārta *pūjā* involved Vedic rites and *mantras*, and worship was performed rather as a duty than as a means of attaining salvation. Many upper-class Hindus still prefer the ways of the Smārtas to Śaiva and Vaiṣṇava forms of worship.

In orthodox brāhmaṇic circles, the brāhmaṇ Śaṅkara, in the ninth century C.E., was propounding a strict monist (Advaita, or nondual) interpretation of sacred Vedāntic scriptures. For him and his followers the only reality was Brahman, the ultimate spirit of the Upaniṣads, with which the individual soul (*ātman*) was identical. All else was simple illusion (*māyā*). He maintained that salvation, or *mukti,* could be attained only by the ascetic mendicant (*sannyāsin*), so he founded an order to train his followers in the proper way to attain salvation through the knowledge of Brahman. It admitted only upper-class men regardless of their stage in life and followed closely the principles of brāhmaṇic orthodoxy. Śaṅkara's Advaita Vedānta is the basis of the philosophical teaching of modern Hindu movements such as the Vedānta Society and Maharishi Mahesh Yogi's Spiritual Regeneration Movement, or TM, both of which are discussed later in this chapter.

The last stage in the evolution of Hinduism, Basham asserts, was principally the result of the influence of the Dravidian culture of southern India from about the eighth to the twelfth centuries.[9] In Tamil Nādu there were new religious movements afoot, characterized by emotionally charged devotionalism. They centred on hymn singers teaching rather in vernacular languages than in Sanskrit, which was known only by the learned.

The most important hymns were written in Tamil by two groups of poets, the Nāyaṉārs, who worshipped Śiva, and the Āḻvārs, who were devotees of Viṣṇu. Their devotional poetry was charged with a mystical fervour and an intense love of their god. The dominant emotion manifested in their poems is joy, which was often outwardly expressed in song and dance. Excerpts from poems addressed to Śiva by two of the greatest Nāyaṉār poets, Appar and Māṇikka Vāśagar, illustrate Tamil devotionalism.

> Though they give me the jewels from Indra's abode,
>   though they grant me dominion o'er earth, yea, o'er heaven,
> if they be not the friend of our Lord Mahādev [Śiva],
>   what care I for wealth by such ruined hand given?
> But if they love Śiva, who hides in his hair
>   the river of Ganges, then whoe'er they be,
> foul lepers, or outcastes, yea, slayers of kine,
>   to them is my homage, gods are they to me.[10]

He whom the King of Gods knows but in part, the God of
 Gods,
 the Triple Lord, who makes, preserves and ends
the lovely universe, the Primal Form,
 the Ancient of Days, the Lord of Pārvatī, . . .
came in his grace and took me for his own,
 so now I bow to none, and revere him alone.
I am among the servants of his servants,
 and I shall bathe in joy, and dance and sing.[11]

The southern Indian popular religion spread northward, where it combined with the Sanskrit Purāṇic tradition and led to the growth of devotional *bhakti* during this time. A product of this commingling of traditions is the *Bhāgavata Purāṇa*, written in the south in the tenth century. Kṛṣṇa is the focus of the entire tenth book, where, for the first time, his sporting with the *gopīs* is given great emphasis. The book presents a fully developed doctrine of the *avatāras* of Viṣṇu, enumerated as twenty-two.

The most important Tamil Śaiva sect was the Śaiva Siddhānta, which in the thirteenth century gave theological and ritual expression to the devotional hymns of the Nāyaṉārs. It emphasized divine grace and the distinction between the God and the self.

The synthesis of popular devotionalism and brāhmaṇic authority found its expression in the southern Indian savant Rāmānuja, who lived in the eleventh to twelfth centuries and founded the Śrīvaiṣṇava sect. Writing commentaries on the major Vedāntic works, he argued directly against Śaṅkara's monist doctrine. He favoured a theistic interpretation of these scriptures, emphasizing the importance of *bhakti* in his system of qualified nondualism (*Vaśiṣṭādvaita*).

In the north, a monist school of Śaivism appeared in Kashmīr in the ninth century. Its system resembled Śaṅkara's but attributed personality to the absolute spirit, conceived to be Śiva rather than the impersonal Brahman.

This period also witnessed, among Śaiva sects, the rise in importance of Śakti, the feminine aspect of Śiva, who had already made herself felt as early as the fourth century with the cult of Durgā, Śiva's consort. The cults devoted to the worship of Śakti in her various manifestations were known as the Śāktas. Whether as the fierce Kālī (Dark One), or as Śiva's wife, Pārvatī or Umā, she is the creative power of Śiva and the object of worship in temples devoted to the reverence of the Devī (Goddess). The deification of the female gave a new and important image to women. The Śākta cults united with esoteric and ascetic tantric groups of the northeast to produce a bizarre form of worship that breached the usual Hindu taboos. As Basham explains, "Small groups of initiates met at night, often in a temple or private house, but also frequently in a burning-ground, among the bones of the dead. The group formed a circle, seated around the circumference of a large circular magic diagram (*yantra, maṇḍala*) drawn on the ground. Though the members of the circle might include brāhmaṇs as well as outcasts, there was no class distinction at the ceremony. . . . After regular evening worship, the propitiation of ghosts, and other rites, the group would indulge in the five M's: *madya* (alcoholic drink), *māṃsa* (meat), *matsya* (fish), *mudrā* (symbolic hand gesture), and *maithuna* (sexual intercourse). The rites concluded with the worship of the five elements [earth, air, fire, water, and ether], to which the five M's corresponded. Among some tantric groups the last of the five M's involved promiscuous copulation, while the members of others brought their wives to the circle."[12] The women in this ritual copulation, it should be pointed out, was not a common prostitute. She had the status of a divinity with whom alone the male devotee could attain a mystical and sacred union. The deification of one chosen female symbolically led to the divinization of the other women present, with whom their male partners might hope also to attain the same spiritual union. Sexual impulses were not restrained, as in other ascetic traditions, but were exploited to reach salvation. Such tantric groups still exist in South Asia, mostly in modern Bengal. They tend to be very secretive, with esoteric doctrines known only to the initiated.

Hinduism reached the apogee of its development by the end of the fourteenth century of the common era. It may be characterized as a theistic or sectarian form of religion with, in certain instances, a strong undercurrent of brāhmaṇic orthodoxy. It stressed temple or domestic worship of a deity (*pūjā*) and was strongly flavoured with devotionalism (*bhakti*). With the exception perhaps of *pūjā*, most of its elements already existed in the classical form represented by the *Bhagavad-gītā*.

Subsequent developments in Hinduism are offshoots of this characteristic form and are indicative of its ability to assimilate and adapt to change. In the late fifteenth and early sixteenth centuries, different elements of Bengali Vaiṣṇavism were brought together by Caitanya, whose sect characterizes much of Bengal's Hinduism. After an intense religious experience at the age of twenty-two, Caitanya established an order whose members expressed their fervent devotion through ecstatic dancing and hymn singing (*saṃkīrtana*), often taking the form of processions through the streets. A modern outgrowth of this movement is A. C. Bhaktivedānta's International Society for Krishna Consciousness (ISKCON), or the Hare Krishnas, whose religious devotionalism can be witnessed in most of the world's major cities.

About the same time as Caitanya, Nānak combined elements of Islām and Christianity with Hindu theology to produce a new religion called Sikhism, which is strongest today in northwestern India but has filtered to other parts of India and the Western world.

In the nineteenth and twentieth centuries, various Hindu reform movements integrated new ideas into the fabric of Hinduism. They gave rise to social reforms in India, such as the abolition of the ancient practice of widow burning (*satī*),[13] child marriages of daughters, and the denial of widows' remarriage—all of which have been accepted to varying degrees—and to the growth of interest in Hinduism in the West. Among the earliest of these movements to reach the West was the Hinduism of the Bengali mystic Rāmakṛṣṇa, a devotee of the goddess Kālī. After having an intense vision of the divine mother, he attracted a small group of followers who preached his simple doctrine that all religions have a valid claim to truth. After Rāmakṛṣṇa's death, the leadership of the movement went to his disciple Vivekānanda, who was instrumental in bringing Hinduism to the West. In 1893 he attended the World's Parliament of Religions in Chicago where his speeches on Hinduism made a deep impression on the delegates. He subsequently lectured in the United States and England and established the Vedānta Society with a permanent group of followers. On his return to India in 1897 he founded the Rāmakṛṣṇa Mission, the most important modern organization of reformed Hinduism. The Vedānta Society now has numerous temples in the West, many of which have monasteries where monks and nuns of the Rāmakṛṣṇa Order carry on the teachings and perform services of the society.

The teachings of Aurobindo Ghose, or Śrī Aurobindo (1872–1950), have attracted the attention of many Western intellectuals. Trained in Classics at Cambridge, Aurobindo began his career with political aspirations. His subversive activities in India led to his arrest in 1908. He was tried for sedition and sent to prison for a year. After his release he fled to what was then the French colony of Pondichéry, south of Madras, where he became an ascetic and founded an *āśraṁ*, retreat, for the study of yoga. His numerous writings reflect his erudition and deep personal understanding of Hindu mysticism and yoga.

More recently the writings of Jiddu Krishnamurti (1895–1986) have been widely read in the West. He taught a deeply individual form of religious involvement through which self-realization is attained by introspection and the renunciation of personal ambition. He rejected organized religion and claimed no special spiritual or mystical skills.

Finally the Spiritual Regeneration Movement of Maharishi

Mahesh Yogi, commonly known as TM (Transcendental Meditation), has recruited many members in the United States and Europe. Stressing the general benefits of meditation, it combines training in meditation with a form of neo-Hindu teaching based on Śaṅkara's Advaita Vedānta. It has promoted research in meditation and its effects and has begun to establish medical clinics to treat patients by a modified and simplified form of traditional Indian medicine known as *āyurveda*, or the science of longevity, which aims to restore a balance to the human body through a variety of naturally based therapies.

Hinduism in the modern age is characterized by its adaptability. Using a foundation of classical Hindu thought and practice, Hindus of all types are adjusting to their present time and place. This flexibility and openness, while following the age-old traditions and teachings of the sages, will permit Hinduism to remain one of the world's major religious forces in the future.

Our survey of Hinduism has focussed on the origin and development of the classical tradition, for it is the bedrock on which all later forms are built. We have examined the available sources to piece together a jigsaw puzzle (to use Basham's analogy) of classical Hinduism, represented in the *Bhagavad-gītā*. Using this picture of it, we looked briefly at the trends and developments that have taken place from the early centuries of the common era to the present. As we encounter the numerous present forms of Hinduism and others that will surely in the future find fertile ground in the West, we shall be better able to understand them if we bear in mind the classical system from which they originated.

Appendix: The Principal Works of A. L. Basham

This bibliography of publications by A. L. Basham represents his most significant contributions to South Asian history and culture and includes works on both Hinduism and Buddhism. Most of the items derive from a bibliography compiled by S. N. Mukherjee and published in *India, History and Thought: Essays in Honour of A. L. Basham*, edited by S. N. Mukherjee (Calcutta: Subarnarekha, 1982), pages 326–31. The works listed here provide the basis for an understanding of Basham's thought and his approach to the study of Indian history and culture.

Books

History and Doctrines of the Ājīvikas. London: Luzac & Co., 1952. Rpt. with new preface. Delhi: Motilal Banarsidass, 1982.

The Wonder That Was India: Survey of the Culture of the Indian Sub-Continent Before the Coming of the Muslims. New York: Grove Press, Inc., 1954. 2d ed. New York: Hawthorn Books, 1963. 3d ed. 1967. Paperback editions published in England, the United States, and India. Translations in French, Polish, Tamil, Sinhalese, and Hindī, with German and Spanish translations projected.

The Indian Sub-Continent in Historical Perspective. Inaugural Lecture. London: School of Oriental and African Studies, 1958. Translated into German by F. Wilhelm, *Saeculum* 10:196–207.

Studies in Indian History and Culture. Calcutta: Sambodhi Publications, 1964.

Aspects of Ancient Indian Culture. Bombay: Asia Publishing House, 1968.

La Civilisation de l'Inde ancienne. Les grandes civilisations. Paris: Arthaud, 1976.

Edited Volumes

Papers on the Date of Kaniṣka, Submitted to the Conference on the Date of Kaniṣka, London, 20–23 April 1960. Leyden: E. J. Brill, 1968.

The Civilizations of Monsoon Asia. Sydney: Angus & Robertson, 1974.

A Cultural History of India. Oxford: Clarendon Press, 1975. Updated ed. of G. T. Garratt's *Legacy of India,* 1937.

Kingship in Asia and Pre-Columbian America. Proceedings of a seminar held at the International Congress of Asianists, Mexico, 1976. Edited and with three chapters by A. L. Basham. Mexico: El Colegio de México. Forthcoming.

Contributions in Edited Volumes

"The Background of Buddhism." In *Man in His Relationships,* edited by H. Westmann, 79–90. London: Routledge & Kegan Paul, 1955.

"Jainism and Buddhism." In *Sources of Indian Tradition,* edited by W. Theodore de Bary, vol. 1, 37–202. New York: Columbia University Press, 1958.

"Hinduism" and "Jainism." In *Concise Encyclopaedia of Living Faiths,* edited by R. C. Zaehner, 225–66. Boston: Beacon Press, 1959.

"The Kashmīr Chronicle" and "Modern Historians of India." In *Historians of India, Pakistan and Ceylon,* edited by C. H. Philips, 57–65, 260–93. London: Oxford University Press, 1961.

"Indian Dawn Poems." In *Eos,* edited by A. T. Hatto, 140–47, 161–75. The Hague: Mouton, 1965.

"Ancient Indian Ideas of Time and History." In *Prāchyavidyā-Taraṅginī,* Golden Jubilee Volume of the Department of Ancient Indian History and Culture, Calcutta University, 49–63. Calcutta: Calcutta University, 1969.

"Traditional Influences on the Thought of Mahatma Gandhi." In *Essays on Gandhian Politics,* edited by R. Kumar, 17–42. Oxford: Clarendon Press, 1971.

"India." In *The Emergence of Man in Society.* Vol. 1, book 4.1, *Civilization,* 427–66. Del Mar, Calif.: CRM Books, 1973.

"History of Hinduism." In *Encyclopaedia Britannica,* vol. 8 (*Macropaedia*), 907–20. 15th ed., 1974.

"The Practice of Medicine in Ancient and Medieval India." In *Asian Medical Systems,* edited by Charles Leslie, 18–43. Berkeley: University of California Press, 1976.

"Some Reflections in the Separate Kaliṅga Edicts of Aśoka." In *Buddhism and Jainism,* edited by H. C. Das, C. Das, and S. R. Pal, 1–7. Cuttack, Orissa, India: Institute of Oriental and Orissan Studies, 1976.

"Indien." In *Krankheit, Heilkunst und Heilung,* edited by H. Schipperges, E. Seidler, and P. U. Unschuld, 145–78. Freiburg: Verlag Karl Alber, 1978.

"Hinduism." In *Encyclopedia of Bioethics,* edited by Warren T. Reich et al., vol. 2, 661–67. New York: The Free Press, 1978.

"Āryan and Non-Āryan in South Asia." In *Āryan and Non-Āryan in India,* edited by Madhav M. Deshpande and Peter Edwin Hook, 1–9. Ann Arbor, Mich.: Center for South and Southeast Asian Studies, 1979.

"The Background to the Rise of Buddhism." In *Studies in History of Buddhism,* edited by A. K. Narain, 13–31. Delhi: B. R. Publishing Corp., 1980.

"Early Imperial India." In *The Encyclopedia of Ancient Civilizations,* edited by Arthur Cotterell, 184–91. London: Rainbird, 1980.

"The Evolution of the Concept of the Bodhisattva." In *The Bodhisattva Doctrine in Buddhism,* edited by Leslie S. Kawamura, 19–59. Waterloo, Ont.: Canadian Corporation for Studies in Religion, Wilfred Laurier University Press, 1981.

Introduction and "The Mandasor Inscription of the Silk-Weavers." In *Essays on Gupta Culture,* edited by Bardwell L. Smith, 1–13, 93–105. Delhi: Motilal Banarsidass, 1983.

"Emperor Aśoka." In *Indological Studies: Prof. D. C. Sirkar Commemoration Volume,* edited by S. K. Maity and Upendra Thakur, 1–5. New Delhi: Abhinav Publications, 1987.

"Religious Concept of Emperor Aśoka." Published posthumously in *Studies in Orientology: Essays in Memory of Prof. A. L. Basham,* edited by S. K. Maity et al., 64–70. Agra, India: Y. K. Publishers, 1988.

Articles

"Harṣa of Kashmīr and the Iconoclast Ascetics." *Bulletin of the School of Oriental and African Studies* 12 (1948): 688–91.

"Recent Work on the Indus Civilization." *Bulletin of the School of Oriental and African Studies* 13 (1949): 140–45.

"Notes on Seafaring in Ancient India." *Art and Letters* (London), 1949:60–71.

"Ajātasattu's War with the Licchavis." *Proceedings of the Indian Historical Congress* 14 (1951): 37–41.

"Prince Vijaya and the Aryanization of Ceylon." *Ceylon Historical Journal* 1 (1952): 163–71.

"A New Study of the Śaka-Kuṣāṇa Period." *Bulletin of the School of Oriental and African Studies* 15 (1953): 80–97.

"The Background to the Rise of Parakkama Bāhu I." *Ceylon Historical Journal* 4 (1955): 10–22.

"The Date of the End of the Reign of Kumāra Gupta I and the Succession After His Death." *Bulletin of the School of Oriental and African Studies* 17 (1955): 366–69.

The Succession of the Line of Kaniṣka." *Bulletin of the School of Oriental and African Studies* 20 (1957): 77–88.

"A New Interpretation of Indian History." *Journal of the Economic and Social History of the Orient* 1 (1958): 333–47.

"Paliad Plates of Bhīmadeva I, v.s. 1112." *Epigraphia Indica* 23 (1959): 235–37.

"Some Reflections on Dravidians and Āryans." *Bulletin of the Institute of Traditional Cultures* (Madras) 2 (1963): 225–34.

"Ancient Indian Kingship." *Indica* (Bombay) 1 (1964): 119–27.

"Buddhism." *The Listener* (London) 72 (1964): 936–40.

"Indian Society and the Legacy of the Past." *Australian Journal of Politics and History* 12, no. 2 (August 1966): 131–45.

"Indian Thought and the West." *Hemisphere* (Canberra), December 1966:7–14.

"The Rise of Buddhism in Its Historical Context." *Asian Studies* (Quezon City), December 1966:395–411.

"La vida social de la India anigua." *Estudios Orientales* (Mexico) 8 (December 1966): 24–36.

"The Mahābhārata and the Rāmāyaṇa." *Unesco Courier,* December 1967:4–10.

"The Pāli Jātakas." *East Wind* (Canberra), 1968–69:1–12.

"Facing Buddhism." *Annals* (Sydney) 80 (1969): 18–21.

"The Ajaṇṭā Murals." *Art and Australia* (Sydney) 8 (1970): 242–51.

"Ājīvikism, a Vanished Indian Religion." *Bulletin of the Ramakrishna Institute* (Calcutta) 23 (1971): 107–17.

"Hindi and Urdu Literature." *Hemisphere* (Canberra), January 1971:24–27.

"India's Contribution to Modern Sciences." *Bhavan's Journal* 19 (1971): 1–16.

"Gupta Style." *Hemisphere* (Canberra), October 1975:18–24.

"Saṃbodhi in Aśoka's Eighth Rock Edict." *Journal of the International Association of Buddhist Studies* 2, no. 1 (1979): 81–83.

"Aśoka and Buddhism—A Re-examination." *Journal of the International Association of Buddhist Studies* 5, no. 1 (1982): 131–43.

Notes

INTRODUCTION

1. A. L. Basham, *The Wonder That Was India* (New York: Grove Press, 1959), 233. The term *Hindu* is of Persian origin, derived from *Sindhu,* the Indian word for the Indus River. It was then passed on to the Greeks, who understood the entirety of India by the name of the river. The Persian term was again employed by the Muslim invaders of the tenth century C.E., who called the country Hindustān; those of its inhabitants who practised the traditional religion were known as Hindus (ibid., 1 n.).

2. At least one videotape of the lectures is available at the Learning Support Services of the University of Wisconsin, Madison (274 Van Hise Hall, University of Wisconsin, Madison, Wis. 53705). It is catalogued under "Civilization of India (Basham)," AS 2.018.01–05, dated 4/9/85–4/10/85.

3. Based on the methodology established by the German schools of classical philology, Indology has traditionally encompassed the detailed philological and linguistic analysis of Indian literary remains. In many parts of Europe this remains the focus of Indological studies. More progressive approaches, from which Basham's methodology is derived, have combined a firm basis in text and language with general historical and cultural studies. For a witty discussion of Basham's historical methodology, one should read W. H. Mcleod's article "History: 'An Academic Amusement,'" in S. K. Maity, et al., eds., *Studies in Or-*

ientology: Essays in Memory of Prof. A. L. Basham (Agra, India: Y. K. Publishers, 1988), 90–94.

Chapter One: The Beginnings of Religion in South Asia

1. Since this site is in Pakistān we use the official spelling of the Pakistān government. More often it is referred to as Mohenjo-dāro, according to the spelling of the former British government of India.

2. A dome-shaped mound covered with masonry. For the Buddhists this was a sacred symbol, recalling the Buddha's death.

3. Much discussion and debate has gone on about the interpretation of this enigmatic figure found on only three seals from the Indus valley. But no view has won general acceptance. For some interesting recent ideas on the problem, see in particular Alf Hiltebeitel, "The Indus Valley 'Proto-Śiva,' Reexamination Through Reflection on the Goddess, the Buffalo, and the Symbolism of *vāhanas,*" *Anthropos* 73, nos. 5–6 (1978): 767–79, and three articles by Doris Srinivasan, "The So-Called Proto-Śiva Seal from Mohenjo-dāro. An Iconological Assessment," *Archives of Asian Art* 29 (1975–76): 47–58; "Vedic Rudra-Śiva," *Journal of the American Oriental Society* 103, no. 3 (1983): 543–56; and "Unhinging Śiva from the Indus Civilization," *Journal of the Royal Asiatic Society of Great Britain and Ireland,* 1984, no. 1: 77–89.

4. Pandits (Sanskrit *paṇḍita*) are traditional Sanskrit scholars who to this day learn vast quantities of Sanskrit works by the time-honoured method of memorization. They achieve higher ranks by memorizing more texts. The highest rank a pandit, who is always male, can reach is *ācārya,* which is equivalent to a doctor in the West.

5. See especially F. Max Müller, *Lectures on the Origin and Growth of Religion, as Illustrated by the Religions of India* (London: Longmans, Green & Co., 1878). Not all scholars of religion follow this interpretation. See in particular Louis Renou, *Religions of Ancient India* (New York: Schocken Books, 1968), 12.

6. This may point to another infiltration of ideas from the Middle East. There are similarities between the myth of Indra slaying the water restrained by demon Vṛtra and the legend of Marduk destroying the forces of chaos led by the sea goddess Ti'amat in the famous Babylonian *Epic of Creation.*

7. See R. Gordon Wasson, *Soma: Divine Mushroom of Immortality* (New York: Harcourt Brace Jovanovich, 1970). Wasson's arguments for the identification of soma with the fly-agaric mushroom are increasingly criticized.

8. *Ṛg-veda* 10.119.2–9. Slightly modified translation by A. L. Basham in *The Wonder That Was India,* 234.

9. Viṣṇu's connection with the sun in the *Ṛg-veda* is rather vague. More specifically, he is known as the "wide-striding one," whose third stride is his highest step, his highest place, beyond the flight of birds or the knowledge of humans. This was his special abode, his heaven. These two, his strides and his heaven, are emphasized in later Hinduism. In the *Ṛg-veda,* he is merely a friend and ally of the powerful war god Indra (cf. Thomas J. Hopkins, *The Hindu Religious Tradition* [Encino, Calif.: Dickenson Publishing, 1972], 12).

Chapter Two: Early Speculations and the Later Sacrificial Cults

1. This is A. L. Basham's translation, free in places, of *Ṛg-veda* 10.129, in *The Wonder That Was India,* 247–48.

2. This is Basham's interpretation of the text. It avoids the illogical situation of the sacrifice of the highest god to himself, who in some mysterious way survived his own death and dismemberment. The latter is the orthodox interpretation. Basham does not dispute the possibility of its being the intention of the poet, but he thinks this unlikely. The poem displays a hard, down-to-earth quality, incompatible with such illogicalities.

3. This is A. L. Basham's partial translation of *Ṛg-veda* 10.90, in *The Wonder That Was India,* 241.

4. The five *saṃhitās* of the *Yajur-veda* differ considerably from one another. Often they are referred to simply by the names of the *saṃhitā* without reference to the *Yajur-veda*. This often leads to confusion among nonspecialists.

5. This is the conventional spelling. If we use *brahma,* we should also have *karma* in place of *karman* and *rājā* in place of *rājan*. The pronunciation without the *n,* which appears only in inflected forms in the original Sanskrit, occurs in the modern languages of northern India.

6. Another class of this literature, which developed from the Brāhmaṇas, is known as the *Śrauta Sūtras*. They treat the principal sacrifices and some domestic rites, simplified from the Vedic major rituals. The *Śrauta Sūtras* are discussed in more detail in chap. 7.

7. Many passages in the early texts indicate that this was a period when petty chieftains, or *rājans* of tribes, were changing their status and converting themsevles and their lines into kings of a given territory rather than remaining chiefs of tribes.

8. Commonly translated as dice. In fact at this period it was a guessing game played with the nuts called *akṣa,* of which ascetics' rosaries are made. At that time, it was not at all dicing but a combination of chance and skill.

Chapter Three: The Development of Philosophy and the Origin of the Doctrine of Transmigration

1. Karl Jaspers, *The Origin and Goal of History* (London: Routledge & Kegan Paul, 1953).

2. Most Sinologists consider Lao-tsu to be a mythological figure, but the beautiful book ascribed to him, *Tao Te Ching,* is certainly a product of this period.

3. Jaspers's theory is not universally accepted by scholars of religion. His identification of charismatic religious leaders who characterized a transformation in the way human beings perceived the world simply does not fit in every case. Where the identification does fit, no concrete causal connections can be found. His description of the religious traditions characteristic of the axial period, nevertheless, deserve closer scrutiny. Although the Hinduism of the Upaniṣads does not derive from a single religious thinker, their mystical doctrines, taught by ascetics rather than by priests, fall into the pattern of the religions of the axial period.

4. There are as well several noncanonical ones, such as the *Allopaniṣad* (*Allah* plus *Upaniṣad*), which, as its name shows, is a Muslim document. In fact, the process of producing Upaniṣads occurs in the present day.

5. The wearing of the thread symbolizes a second birth, with the thread itself representing the threshold. The one who wears it, the

twice-born, dwells simultaneously in chronological time and in eternity.

6. See especially *Śatapatha Brāhmaṇa* 10.4.3, 10.5.2, and 13.3.5.

7. In Hinduism the status of plants is rather dubious. It is believed by many that vegetable life does not transmigrate, though trees and large plants may be the homes of minor divinities (*vṛkṣadevatā*) like the dryads of classical Greece. The heterodox Jains, on the other hand, maintain that every plant is the home of a soul or a colony of souls and, moreover, that there are souls in rocks, water, and air.

8. Some modern Hindu propagandists declare that the soul of a human being, however wicked, is so far advanced that it cannot descend into an animal body. This idea was started by the Theosophical Society and has been taken up by a few of the Indian teachers who have come to preach a simplified kind of neo-Hinduism to Western audiences. The view is nowhere to be found in any ancient or mediaeval text. The numerous rebirths as animals of the Buddha's 550 rebirths, found in the Jātaka stories, clearly indicate that this idea was not part of the original doctrine of transmigration. One of the favourite imprecations, appended at the end of deeds granting land to brāhmaṇs or temples, was "May he who seeks to resume this grant become a worm in dung for eighty thousand years." Note that this refers not to a single worm but to an immense series of short-lived worms, a fate even more terrible.

9. The notion that transmigration was a non-Āryan importation began with Archibald Gough, who in the first chapter of his *Philosophy of the Upaniṣads and Ancient Indian Metaphysics* (London: Trübner, 1882), claims that transmigration, being something quite new, must have arisen among the indigenous people. More recent speculations about the origin of the doctrine of transmigration link it to the ideas that existed among the śramaṇic, or heterodox, ascetic circles of the seventh and sixth centuries B.C.E. (See in particular Gananath Obeyesekere, "The Rebirth Eschatology and Its Transformations: A Contribution to the Sociology of Early Buddhism," in Wendy D. O'Flaherty, ed., *Karma and Rebirth in Classical Indian Traditions* [Berkeley: University of California Press, 1980], 137–64.)

10. It is repeated twice, with slight variations, in the same Upaniṣad (*Bṛhadāraṇyaka Upaniṣad* 2.4, 4.5).

11. Some have suggested (e.g., Wendy D. O'Flaherty, "Karma and Rebirth in the Vedas and Purāṇas," in Wendy D. O'Flaherty, ed., *Karma and Rebirth in Classical Indian Traditions*, 3–37) that here *kar-*

man simply means the works of orthodox religion, especially sacrifice, and certainly the word is often used in this sense. But if this were Yājñavalkya's intention there would be no point in secrecy, for it was common knowledge that performing sacrifices provided beneficial spiritual results. The idea that every deed might bear results in the future, however, must have been a very new one.

12. Jaivali asked other questions that are not very relevant to the subject of transmigration.

13. These are those who dwell in the World of the Fathers and who are capable of both punishing and blessing.

14. Note that the plant containing the soul must be eaten by a male. We are not told what happens to it if it is eaten by a woman, but since woman is the field in which man sows the seed, and she plays no other part in the formation of the child, it seems that the soul eaten by a woman must be eliminated from her body and enter another plant to await a male eater.

15. R. C. Zaehner translates *buddhi* here as soul, distinct from *ātman* (*Hindu Scriptures* [London: J. M. Dent & Sons, 1966], 176). In later philosophical Sanskrit the word had several shades of meaning, but this is one of the earliest occurrences of the term and we prefer a meaning nearer the original meaning of the root *budh-* to be awake, aware.

16. The other five senses (*jñānedriya*) are hearing, touch, sight, taste, and smell.

17. *Kaṭha Upaniṣad* 3.7–8.

Chapter Four: The Mystical and Ascetic Traditions

1. *Bṛhadāraṇyaka Upaniṣad* 4.4.

2. In ancient India it was believed that all space was filled by a very subtle, uniform substance called *ākāśa*. The concept closely resembles the ether of pre-Einstein physics.

3. Thirteen if we include the *Maitrī Upaniṣad,* which is appreciably later than any of the others but still fairly old.

4. Carved inscriptions appear certainly only in the reign of Aśoka (about 270–232 B.C.E.), but there is good reason to believe that writing on perishable material was known several centuries earlier.

5. *Dīgha Nikāya* 1.55. The translation is by A. L. Basham, in *The Wonder That Was India,* 296.

6. On the status of plant life in the scheme of *saṃsāra,* see chap. 3, n. 7. In general it was agreed that vegetable life was lower in the scale of being than animal life.

7. *Anyatra tīrthebhyaḥ,* "except for sacred places." The *tīrtha* is usually a sacred bathing place by a river. The passage is interpreted by Śaṅkara and others as referring to ritual killing of animals.

8. The whole of the fifteenth chapter of the *Atharva-veda* is devoted to the *vrātyas.*

9. More commonly translated the Enlightened One (the root *budh* means to be awake). The implication of the term seems to have originally been that Siddhārtha was fully awake, while ordinary people were half asleep.

10. For introductory material on Buddhism the reader should refer to A. L. Basham's section on Buddhism in *The Wonder That Was India,* 256–87; Edward Conze, *Buddhist Thought in India* (London: Allen & Unwin, 1962); Richard H. Robinson and Willard L. Johnson, *Buddhist Religion: A Historical Introduction,* 3d ed. (Belmont, Calif.: Wadsworth Publishing Co., 1982); Edward J. Thomas, *The Life of Buddha as Legend and History,* 3d rev. ed. (New York: Barnes & Noble, 1952); and Edward J. Thomas, *The History of Buddhist Thought* (London: Routledge & Kegan Paul, 1959).

11. The comparison between the omniscient *jīva* of Jainism and the monad of Leibniz is close. It seems, however, that any influence of Jainism on the German philosopher was completely impossible.

12. For rulers, soldiers, and policemen violence necessary in defense or to preserve law and order was permitted as an unfortunate necessity in an evil age.

13. In recent times the rule against light has been somewhat relaxed in many monasteries. Electric lights, suitably protected so that moths and other insects cannot be harmed in them, are now often acceptable.

14. Probably the implication of the term *ājīvika* is "those ascetics who took lifelong vows," as opposed to the Buddhists, whose vows could be rescinded without any sense of shame or shortcoming.

15. *Dīgha Nikāya* 1.53–54. Translation is by A. L. Basham, in *The Wonder That Was India,* 295.

16. Though the claim in favour of the middle class is almost as old as the twentieth century (see in particular T. W. Rhys Davids, *Buddhist India* [London: T. Fisher Unwin, 1903]), only recently a careful analysis has been made of the data in the early Buddhist texts in Pāli. The results of this study by Uma Chakravarti (*The Social Dimensions of*

Early Buddhism [Delhi: Oxford University Press, 1987]) are surprising. This table includes only those names for which a class reference was given.

	Monks	Lay Supporters
Brāhmaṇs	39	76
Khattiyas (*Kṣatriyas*)	23	28
Uccākulas / *Gahapatis* } (*Vaiśyas*)	23	58
Nīcakulas (*Śūdras* and Untouchables)	8	11
Paribbājakas (Other Ascetics)	8	7
Totals	101	180

Chapter Five: Orthodoxy and the Epic Tradition

1. The word *sūtra* means thread, and the term was later given to various classes of didactic text written in brief, often elliptical prose sentences especially suited for memorization.

2. Here we must pay tribute to the world's greatest (at least in terms of size) achievement in textual criticism, the critical edition of this anonymous poem, which exists in several recensions and literally thousands of manuscripts. Well before World War II a committee of Sanskritists in the Bhāndārkar Oriental Institute, in Pūṇe, decided to produce a critical edition of the *Mahābhārata*. They examined every manuscript they could trace, whether complete or partial, and produced the critical edition by instalments over a period of about forty years. It is a wonderful achievement of Indian scholarship.

3. In several places the text mentions Hūṇas (Huns), who were hardly known in India until about 450. On the other hand another tribe, the Gurjaras, who appeared in India about 550, is not mentioned.

4. Comments on Vyāsa derive from A. L. Basham, *The Wonder That Was India*, 407, and from Maurice Winternitz, *History of Indian Literature*, vol. 1, 2d ed. (1927; rpt. New Delhi: Oriental Books Reprint Corp., 1977), 323–24.

5. According to the finished story, every people of South Asia took part in the battle, along with many others from outside India, such as the Chinese, the Greeks, and the Śakas, or Scythians, the Central Asian nomads. Probably in fact the battle was a comparably small affair, not apparently important enough to make an impression on the authors of the later Vedic literature, which was being composed around that time.

6. *Sītā* means furrow, and it is evident that in Vedic times there was a minor agricultural goddess of this name.

7. One exception is Rāma's defeat of Vālin, the usurper of the monkey kingdom of Kiṣkindha, by a trick.

8. "Flying through the sky" refers most probably to ascetic or yogic powers.

9. The three worlds are the heavenly realm of the gods, the earthly world of living beings, and the underworld, inhabited by the *nāgas,* or snakes.

10. As Rāma is to go off in the forest and become an ascetic, so also Sītā, as a dutiful wife, will practise the austerities of an ascetic.

11. *Rāmāyaṇa* 2.24 (critical edition). Translation by Sheldon I. Pollock, *The Rāmāyaṇa of Vālmīki: An Epic of Ancient India,* vol. 2, *Ayodhyākāṇḍa* (Princeton: Princeton University Press, 1986), 135–36.

12. There is a tendency in modern India to rationalize the monkeys of the *Rāmāyaṇa* as wild people of the Deccan, having the monkey as their totem. This euhemeristic interpretation has no basis in the text itself, where the monkeys certainly have human intelligence but are otherwise normal monkeys, with hair and tails. Another increasingly popular rationalization is the identification of Laṅkā as a place in Madhya Pradesh, thus adjusting the story to the known archaeological facts of about 1000 B.C.E. This interpretation is equally incredible, since Laṅkā in the *Rāmāyaṇa* is, like modern Śrī Laṅkā, a large island surrounded by the ocean. Moreover, among the other islands visited by Hanumat in his search for Sītā is Yavadvīpa, or Java. The story could have been composed only when Śrī Laṅkā was known in the north.

In fact there is good reason to believe that the *Rāmāyaṇa* as it is at present is the conflation of two stories, one about a righteous prince who was forced to leave his kingdom and the other about a prince who rescued his wife from captivity with the aid of an army of monkeys. The Buddhist version of the story, *Dasaratha Jātaka,* makes no reference to the kidnapping of Sītā or to Rāma's conquest of Laṅkā, and since the early Buddhist monks were always on the lookout for exciting stories to tell to the laity it is unlikely that they had heard the full version as told in the *Rāmāyaṇa*. Buddhist traditions in China have also preserved the tale of an unnamed prince who rescued his wife from a demon with the help of an army of monkeys.

Chapter Six: The Bhagavad-gītā and the Triumph of Theism

1. Discrepancies such as this are explained away by some neo-Hindu propagandists as arising from a lack of full understanding of the text. The logical law of the excluded middle (either *x* or not-*x*) on which Western thinking has been largely based is said to have been proved false by subatomic physics and relativity theory and therefore both of these propositions are true. The logic of this is itself false. Even if the law of the excluded middle is not always valid, this shows only that both these propositions *may* be true. And in any case, the law of the excluded middle conforms with the whole corpus of human experience on the microcosmic level much better than does its negation, for all apparent breaches of the law can be traced back to inadequate terminology or insufficient understanding.

2. On *ākāśa,* see chap. 4, n. 2.

3. *Chāndogya Upaniṣad* 5.3–10; see pp. 46–47.

4. The following verse (9.5) seems to maintain a dualist doctrine: "Beings do not subsist in me. . . . My self creates beings, but it does not subsist in them, it causes them to be."

5. This word in later Advaita philosophy often has the sense of illusion, but the *Bhagavad-gītā* gives no indication of teaching the unreality of the phenomenal world.

Chapter Seven: The Ritual and Dharma Literature and the New Hindu Orthodoxy

1. Cf. chap. 5, n. 1.

2. A *paṇa* or *kārṣāpaṇa* is a basic silver punchmarked coin, weighing 57.8 grains (A. L. Basham, *The Wonder That Was India,* 504).

3. Ibid., 120.

4. Ibid., 121.

5. *Laws of Manu* 5.147 ff., translated by A. L. Basham, in *The Wonder That Was India,* 180–81.

6. This short discussion of women in ancient India is based on A. L. Basham's interesting discussion of women in *The Wonder That Was India,* 177–88. Much research on women in ancient India needs to be done and is currently being undertaken by competent scholars.

7. A. L. Basham, *The Wonder That Was India,* 335.

8. Ibid., 335–36. The *devadāsīs,* holders of a time-honoured position passed on from mother to daughter, also served as temple prostitutes. Rather than being scorned, women in this position were generally looked on with approval. Their appearance in Hindu temples dates from the eighth to the twelfth centuries, but their function was abolished with Hindu reform movements of the nineteenth century.

9. Ibid., 298.

10. Translation of part of a poem by Appar, in R. C. Zaehner, *Hinduism* (Oxford: Oxford University Press, 1970), 132.

11. Translation of part of a poem by Māṇikka Vāśagar, in F. Kingsbury and G. E. Philips, *Hymns of the Tamil Śaivite Saints* (Calcutta, 1921), 93–94. Cited by A. L. Basham, *The Wonder That Was India,* 331.

12. A. L. Basham, *The Wonder That Was India,* 337.

13. The word *satī,* Anglicized to *suttee,* means "a virtuous woman" and refers to a widow's self-immolation on her husband's funeral pyre. Basham dates the origin of the practice to before the time of the *Ṛgveda* (the second millennium B.C.E.) and locates its rise in the ancient Mesopotamian city of Ur, in ancient China, and among some early Indo-European peoples. It is permitted in the early *smṛti* literature but not strongly emphasized. By the sixth century C.E. it was quite common all over India, as evidenced by the numerous *satī* stones commemorating dutiful wives who had joined their slain husbands in death. "Some medieval writers roundly declared that the satī, by her self-immolation, expunges both her own and her husband's sins, and that the two enjoy together 35 million years of bliss in heaven" (A. L. Basham, *The Wonder That Was India,* 188). Although *satī* was voluntary, pressure made it virtually obligatory for certain high-caste, especially *kṣatriya,* widows. Moreover, Indians' general disdain of widows because of the burden they placed on their husbands' families might well have prompted such women to prefer death, in the hope of being reunited with their husbands, to a painful life of shame, poverty, and servitude (ibid.). Much to the chagrin of European observers and cer-

tain progressive Indians, the practice continued to be performed even after it was suppressed in 1829 by government regulation 17. A case of suttee occurred as recently as 1987 in Rājasthān, even though it is a criminal offence to commit or aid the act. The British Indologist Julia Leslie is completing an excellent study of *satī* titled *Path to the Pyre: Satī in its Indological Context*.

Bibliography

In addition to numerous works by A. L. Basham on ancient Indian history, culture, and religion, the following sources will prove valuable in gaining a deeper understanding of the origins of classical Hinduism and its later development. They are divided into broad categories roughly corresponding to the chapters of this book. Each category is further divided into general secondary sources and translated texts. Every effort has been made to include the most recent expositions on the various aspects of Hinduism, while not excluding old standards.

General Sources

Bhattacharyya, Haridas, ed. *The Cultural Heritage of India.* 4 vols. 2d ed., rev. and enl. Calcutta: Ramakrishna Mission, Institute of Culture, 1965.

Brown, W. Norman. *Man in the Universe: Some Cultural Continuities in Indian Thought.* Berkeley: University of California Press, 1970.

Dasgupta, Surendra Nath. *A History of Indian Philosophy.* 5 vols. 1922–55. Rpt. Delhi: Motilal Banarsidass, 1975.

Farquhar, J. N. *An Outline of the Religious Literature of India.* 1920. Rpt. Delhi: Motilal Banarsidass, 1967.

Hopkins, Thomas J. *The Hindu Religious Tradition.* Encino, Calif.: Dickenson Publishing, 1971.

Kosambi, Damodar Dharmanand. *Ancient India: A History of Its Culture and Civilization*. New York: Pantheon Books, 1965.

Maity, S. K., et al., eds. *Studies in Orientology: Essays in Memory of Prof. A. L. Basham*. Agra, India: Y. K. Publishers, 1988.

Majumdar, R. C., and A. D. Pusalkar, eds. *The History and Culture of the Indian People*. 11 vols. Bombay: Bharatiya Vidya Bhavan, 1951–77.

Nilakanta Sastri, Kallidaikurichi Aiyah Aiyar. *History of South India: From Prehistoric Times to the Fall of Vijayanagara*. 2d ed. Bombay: Oxford University Press, 1958.

———. *Development of Religion in South India*. Bombay: Orient Longman, 1963.

Radhakrishnan, Sarvepalli. *Indian Philosophy*. 2 vols. New York: Macmillan, 1927.

Renou, Louis, and Jean Filliozat. *L'Inde classique: manuel des études indiennes*. 2 vols. Paris: Imprimerie Nationale, 1953.

———. *The Nature of Hinduism*. Translated by Patrick Evens. New York: Walker and Co., 1962.

———. *Religions of Ancient India*. Translated by Sheila M. Fynn. New York: Schocken Books, 1968.

Rosenfield, John M. *The Dynastic Arts of the Kuṣāṇas*. Berkeley: University of California Press, 1967.

Staal, Frits. *Exploring Mysticism*. Harmondsworth, Middlesex, England: Penguin Books, 1975.

Thapar, Romila. *Aśoka and the Decline of the Mauryans*. London: Oxford University Press, 1961.

Smith, Vincent A. *The Oxford History of India*. 3d. ed. Oxford: Clarendon Press, 1958.

Zaehner, R. C. *Hinduism*. London: Oxford University Press, 1970.

Anthologies of Texts

De Bary, William Theodore, and Stephen Hay, eds. *Sources of Indian Tradition*. 2 vols. New York: Columbia University Press, 1988.

Edgerton, Franklin. *Beginnings of Indian Philosophy*. Cambridge: Harvard University Press, 1965.

Embree, Ainslie T. *The Hindu Tradition*. New York: Modern Library, 1966.

Radhakrishnan, Sarvepalli, and Charles Moore, eds. *Source Book in Indian Philosophy*. Princeton: Princeton University Press, 1967.

Renou, Louis, comp. *Hinduism*. New York: Braziller, 1961.
Zaehner, R. C. *Hindu Scriptures*. London: J. M. Dent & Sons, 1966.

Prehistoric India

Agrawal, D. P. *The Archaeology of India*. Scandinavian Institute of Asian Studies. Monograph Series, no. 46. London: Curzon Press, 1985.

Allchin, Bridget, and Allchin, Raymond. *The Rise of Civilization in India and Pakistan*. Cambridge World Archaeology. Cambridge: Cambridge University Press, 1982.

Hiltebeitel, Alf. "The Indus Valley "Proto-Śiva," Reexamined Through Reflection on the Goddess, the Buffalo, and the Symbolism of *vāhanas*." *Anthropos* 73, nos. 5–6 (1978): 767–97.

Marshall, Sir John, ed. *Mohenjo-Dāro and the Indus Civilization, Being an Official Account of Archaeological Excavations at Mohenjo-Dāro Carried Out by the Government of India Between the Years 1922 and 1927*. 3 vols. London: Arthur Probsthain, 1931.

Piggott, Stuart. *Prehistoric India*. Harmondsworth, Middlesex, England: Penguin Books, 1959.

Srinivasan, Doris. "The So-Called Proto-Śiva Seal from Mohenjo-dāro: An Iconological Assessment." *Archives of Asian Art* 29 (1975–76): 47–58.

———. "Unhinging Śiva from the Indus Civilization." *Journal of the Royal Asiatic Society of Great Britain and Ireland*, 1984, no. 1: 77–89.

Wheeler, Sir Robert Eric Mortimer. *Early India and Pakistan to Ashoka*. Rev. ed. New York: Praeger, 1968.

Vedic Religion and Ritual

Secondary Sources

Bhattacharji, Sukumari. *The Indian Theogony*. Cambridge: Cambridge University Press, 1970.

Bloomfield, Maurice. *The Religion of the Veda*. New York: Putnam, 1908.

Childe, V. Gordon. *The Āryans: A Study of Indo-European Origins*. New York: Knopf, 1926.

Dandekar, Ramchandra Narayana. *Śrautakoṣa* [Encyclopaedia on Vedic Ritual]. English Section. Based on the Śrautasūtras Belonging to the Various Vedic Schools. Vols. 1–2. Pūṇe, India: Vaidika Śaṃodhana Maṇḍala, 1958–73.

Gonda, Jan. *Vedic Literature (Saṃhitās and Brāhmaṇas)*. A History of Indian Literature, vol. 1, no. 1. Wiesbaden: Otto Harrassowitz, 1975.

———. *The Ritual Sūtras*. A History of Indian Literature, vol. 1, no. 2. Wiesbaden: Otto Harrassowitz, 1977.

Heesterman, Johannes Cornelis. *The Ancient Indian Royal Consecration*. The Hague: Mouton, 1957.

———. *The Inner Conflict of Tradition: Essays in Indian Ritual, Kingship, and Society*. Chicago: University of Chicago Press, 1985.

Hubert, Henri, and Marcel Mauss. *Sacrifice: Its Nature and Function*. Translated by W. D. Halls. Chicago: University of Chicago Press, 1964.

Kane, Pandurang V. *History of Dharmaśāstra*. 5 vols. Pūṇe, India: Bhāndārkar Oriental Research Institute, 1930–62.

Keith, Arthur Berriedale. *The Religion and Philosophy of the Veda and Upanishads*. Harvard Oriental Series, nos. 31–32. 1925. Rpt. Delhi: Motilal Banarsidass, 1970.

Knipe, David M. *In the Image of Fire: Vedic Experience of Heat*. Delhi: Motilal Banarsidass, 1975.

Macdonell, Arthur A. *Vedic Mythology*. 1898. Rpt. Delhi: Motilal Banarsidass, 1974.

Müller, F. Max. *Lectures on the Origin and Growth of Religion, As Illustrated by the Religions of India*. The Hibbert Lectures. London: Longman, Green & Co., 1878.

Santucci, James A. *An Outline of Vedic Literature*. Missoula, Mont.: Scholars Press, 1976.

Schmidt, Hanns-Peter. "The Origin of Ahiṃsā." In *Mélanges d'Indianisme: à la mémoire de Louis Renou*, 626–55. Paris: Editions E. de Boccard, 1968.

Srinivasin, Doris M. "Vedic Rudra-Śiva." *Journal of the American Oriental Society* 103, no. 3 (1983): 543–56.

Wasson, R. Gordon *Soma: Divine Mushroom of Immortality*. New York: Harcourt Brace Jovanovich, 1970.

See also "General Sources," especially those sections of works relating to Vedic religion and ritual.

Translated Texts

Bloomfield, Maurice, trans. *Hymns of the Atharva-Veda*. Sacred Books of the East, no. 42. 1897. Rpt. Delhi: Motilal Banarsidass, 1973.

Eggeling, Julius, trans. *The Śatapatha-Brāhmaṇa According to the Text of the Mādhyandina School*. Sacred Books of the East, nos. 12, 26, 41, 43, 44. 1882–1900. Rpt. Delhi: Motilal Banarsidass, 1972.

Geldner, Karl Friedrich, trans. *Der Rig-Veda*. Harvard Oriental Series, nos. 33–36. Cambridge: Harvard University Press, 1951.

Griffith, Ralph T. H., trans. *The Hymns of the Ṛgveda*. 2 vols. 1896–97. Rpt. Varanasi, India: Chowkhamba Sanskrit Series Office, 1971.

Keith, Arthur Berriedale, trans. *The Veda of the Black Yajus School Entitled the Taittirīya Sanhitā*. Harvard Oriental Series, nos. 18–19. 1914. Rpt. Delhi: Motilal Banarsidass, 1967.

———, trans. *Rigveda Brāhmaṇas: The Aitareya and Kauṣītaki Brāhmaṇas of the Rigveda*. Harvard Oriental Series, no. 25. 1920. Rpt. Delhi: Motilal Banarsidass, 1971.

Maurer, Walter H., trans. *Pinnacles of India's Past: Selections from the Ṛgveda*. University of Pennsylvania, Studies on South Asia, no. 2. Amsterdam and Philadelphia: John Benjamins Publishing Co., 1986.

Müller, F. Max, and Hermann Oldenberg, trans. *Vedic Hymns*. Sacred Books of the East, nos. 32, 46. 1891, 1897. Rpt. Delhi: Motilal Banarsidass, 1973.

O'Flaherty, Wendy D., trans. *The Rig-Veda: An Anthology*. Harmondsworth, Middlesex, England: Penguin Books, 1981.

Oldenberg, Hermann, and F. Max Müller, trans. *The Gṛhya-Sūtras: Rules of Vedic Domestic Ceremonies*. Sacred Books of the East, nos. 29–30. 1886, 1892. Rpt. Delhi: Motilal Banarsidass, 1973.

Whitney, William Dwight, trans., Charles Rockwell Lanman, ed. *Atharva-Veda-Saṃhitā*. Harvard Oriental Series, nos. 7–8. 1905. Rpt. Delhi: Motilal Banarsidass, 1971.

Zysk, Kenneth G., trans. *Religious Healing in the Veda with Translations and Annotations of Medical Hymns from the "Ṛgveda" and the "Atharvarveda" and Renderings from the Corresponding Ritual Texts*. Transactions of the American Philosophical Society, vol. 75, no. 7. Philadelphia: The Society, 1985.

See also the translations of Vedic texts listed in "Anthologies of Texts," under "General Sources."

Early Philosophy, Transmigration, and Asceticism

Secondary Sources

Chakravarti, Uma. *The Social Dimensions of Early Buddhism*. Delhi: Oxford University Press, 1987.

Conze, Edward. *Buddhist Thought in India*. London: Allen & Unwin, 1962.

Davids, Thomas W. Rhys. *Buddhist India*. London: T. Fisher Unwin, 1903.

Eliade, Mircea. *Yoga: Immortality and Freedom*. Translated by Willard Trask. 2d ed. rev. and enl. Princeton: Princeton University Press, 1969.

Gough, Archibald E. *The Philosophy of the Upaniṣads and Ancient Indian Metaphysics*. 3d ed. London: Trübner, 1903.

Jaspers, Karl. *The Origin and Goal of History*. London: Routledge & Kegan Paul, 1953.

O'Flaherty, Wendy D., ed. *Karma and Rebirth in Classical Indian Traditions*. Berkeley: University of California Press, 1980.

Robinson, Richard H., and Willard L. Johnson. *Buddhist Religion: A Historical Introduction*. 3d ed. Belmont, Calif.: Wadsworth Publishing Co., 1982.

Thomas, Edward J. *The Life of Buddha as Legend and History*. 3d rev. ed. New York: Barnes & Noble, 1952.

———. *The History of Buddhist Thought*. London: Routledge & Kegan Paul,1959.

See also works on Indian religious and philosophical thought under "General Sources" and A. B. Keith's *The Religion and Philosophy of the Veda and Upanishads,* 2 vols.

Translated Texts

Hume, Robert Ernest, trans. *The Thirteen Principal Upanishads*. 2d rev. ed. New York: Oxford University Press, 1971.

Keith, Arthur Berriedale, trans. *The Śāṅkhāyana Āraṇyaka*. London: Royal Asiatic Society, 1908.

———, trans. *The Aitareya Āraṇyaka* Oxford: Clarendon Press, 1909.

Radhakrishnan, Sarvepalli, trans. *The Principal Upanishads*. London: Allen & Unwin, 1953.

See also translated excerpts from the Upaniṣads in "Anthologies of Texts," under "General Sources."

Epics

Secondary Sources

Brockington, J. L. *Righteous Rāma: The Evolution of an Epic.* Delhi: Oxford University Press, 1984.

Vyas, Shantikumar Nanooram. *India in the Rāmāyaṇa Age: A Study of the Social and Cultural Conditions in Ancient India as Described in Vālmīki's Rāmāyaṇa.* Delhi: Atma Ram, 1967.

See also works under "General Sources," especially those sections dealing with the *Mahābhārata* and *Rāmāyaṇa.*

Translated Texts

Dutt, M. N., trans. *Mahābhārata.* 18 vols. Calcutta: Elysium Press, 1895–1905.

Ganguly, K. M., trans., P. C. Roy, ed. *The Mahābhārata.* 12 vols. Rpt. Calcutta: Oriental Publishing Company, 1952.

Goldman, Robert P., and Sally J. Sutherland. *The Rāmāyaṇa of Vālmīki: An Epic of Ancient India.* Vol. 1, *Bālakāṇḍa.* Princeton Library of Asian Translations. Princeton: Princeton University Press, 1984.

Pollock, Sheldon I., trans., Robert P. Goldman, ed. *The Rāmāyaṇa of Vālmīki: An Epic of Ancient India.* Vol. 2, *Ayodhyākāṇḍa.* Princeton Library of Asian Translations. Princeton: Princeton University Press, 1986.

Shastri, Hari Prasad, trans. *The Rāmāyaṇa of Vālmīki.* 3 vols. London: Shanti Sadan, 1952–59.

Van Buitenen, J. A. B., ed. and trans. *The Mahābhārata.* Vols. 1–3. Chicago: University of Chicago Press, 1973–78 (incomplete).

See also translated excerpts from the epics in certain "Anthologies of Texts," under "General Sources."

The "Bhagavad-gītā"

Secondary Sources

See "General Sources," especially sections of works that deal with the *Bhagavad-gītā,* and discussions of the text and religion found in the translations that follow.

Translated Texts

Edgerton, Franklin, trans. *The Bhagavad Gītā.* Cambridge: Harvard University Press, 1972.
Radhakrishnan, Sarvepalli, trans. *The Bhagavadgītā.* 2d ed. 1967. Rpt. New York: Harper & Row, 1973.
Zaehner, R. C., trans. *The Bhagavad-gītā.* London: Oxford University Press, 1969.

Numerous translations of the *Bhagavad-gītā* exist. These three, however, present the text from three distinct points of view: Western philology, Advaita Vedānta, and Christian theology, respectively. They should be compared to each other to obtain an understanding of the range of possible interpretations of one important Hindu scripture.

Hindu Law

Secondary Sources

Auboyer, Jeannine. *Daily Life in Ancient India, from Approximately 200 B.C. to A.D. 700.* London: Asia Publishing House, 1965.
Banerji, Sures Chandra. *Dharma-Sūtras: A Study of Their Origin and Development.* Calcutta: Punthi Pastak, 1962.
Derrett, J. Duncan M. *Religion, Law and the State in India.* London: Faber and Faber, 1968.
———. *Dharmaśāstra and Juridical Literature.* A History of Indian Literature, vol. 4, no. 1. Wiesbaden: Otto Harrassowitz, 1978.
Gonda, Jan. *Ancient Indian Kingship from the Religious Point of View.* Leyden: E. J. Brill, 1966.
Lingat, Robert. *The Classical Law of India.* Translated by J. Duncan M. Derrett. Berkeley: University of California Press, 1973.

See also "General Sources," especially sections of works that deal with Hindu law (*dharma*), and P. V. Kane's *History of Dharmaśāstra, 5* vols.

Translated Texts

Bühler, Georg, trans. *The Sacred Laws of the Āryas.* Sacred Books of the East, nos. 2, 14. 1879, 1882. Rpt. Delhi: Motilal Banarsidass, 1975.

———, trans. *The Laws of Manu.* Sacred Books of the East, no. 25. 1886. Rpt. Delhi: Motilal Banarsidass, 1975.

Jolly, Julius, trans. *The Institutes of Vishṇu.* Sacred Books of the East, no. 7. 1880. Rpt. Delhi: Motilal Banarsidass, 1970.

———, trans. *The Minor Law Books.* Sacred Books of the East, no. 33. 1889. Rpt. Delhi: Motilal Banarsidass, 1969.

See also translated excerpts from the Hindu law books cited in "Anthologies of Texts," under "General Sources."

Women in Hinduism

Altekar, Anant Sadashiv. *The Position of Women in Ancient Hindu Civilization from Ancient Times to the Present Day.* 3d ed. Delhi: Motilal Banarsidass, 1983.

Hawley, John Stratton, and Donna Marie Wulff, eds. *The Divine Consort: Rādhā and the Goddesses of India.* Boston: Beacon Press, 1987.

Kinsley, David. *Hindu Goddesses: Visions of the Divine Feminine in the Hindu Religious Tradition.* Berkeley: University of California Press, 1976.

Meyer, Johann J. *Sexual Life in Ancient India.* New York: Barnes & Noble Books, 1953.

Pinkham, Mildred Worth. *Women in the Sacred Scriptures of Hindus.* New York: Columbia University Press, 1941.

Purāṇas and Hindu Mythology

Secondary Sources

Bailey, Greg. *The Mythology of Brahmā.* Delhi: Oxford University Press, 1983.

Courtright, Paul B. *Gaṇeśa: Lord of Obstacles, Lord of Beginnings.* New York and London: Oxford University Press, 1985.

Dawson, John. *A Classical Dictionary of Hindu Mythology.* 12th ed. London: Routledge & Kegan Paul, 1972.

Hazra, R. C. *Studies in the Purāṇic Records of Hindu Rites and Customs*. Decca: University of Decca, 1940.

Hopkins, E. Washburn. *Epic Mythology*. 1915. Rpt. Delhi: Motilal Banarsidass, 1986.

Kinsley, David R. *The Sword and the Flute, Kālī and Kṛṣṇa: Dark Visions of the Terrible and the Sublime in Hindu Mythology*. Berkeley: University of California Press, 1973.

O'Flaherty, Wendy D. *Asceticism and Eroticism in the Mythology of Śiva*. New York and London: Oxford University Press, 1973.

———. *The Origins of Evil in Hindu Mythology*. Berkeley: University of California Press, 1976.

Preciado-Solis, Benjamin. *The Kṛṣṇa Cycle in the Purāṇas*. Delhi: Motilal Banarsidass, 1984.

Rocher, Ludo. *The Purāṇas*. A History of Indian Literature, vol. 2, no. 3. Wiesbaden: Otto Harrassowitz, 1986.

Sheth, Noel. *The Divinity of Krishna*. Delhi: Munshiram Manoharlal, 1984.

See also "General Sources," especially sections of works that deal with the Purāṇas and Hindu mythology.

Translated Texts

Bhattacharya, A. B., trans., A. S. Gupta, ed. *Kūrma Purāṇa*. Varanasi, India: All India Kashiraj Trust, 1972.

Dimmitt, Cornelia, and J. A. B. van Buitenen, trans. *Classical Hindu Mythology: A Reader in the Sanskrit Purāṇas*. Philadelphia: Temple University Press, 1978.

Dutt, M. N., trans. *Harivaṃśa* [*Purāṇa*]. Calcutta: Elysium Press, 1897.

———, trans. *Agni Purāṇa*. Rpt. Varanasi, India: Chowkhamba Sanskrit Series Office, 1967.

Mukhopadhyaya, S. M., trans. *Vāmana Purāṇa*. Varanasi, India: All India Kashiraj Trust, 1968.

O'Flaherty, Wendy D., trans. *Hindu Myths*. Baltimore: Penguin Books, 1975.

Pargiter, F. E., trans. *Mārkaṇḍeya Purāṇa*. Calcutta: Asiatic Society, 1904.

Sanyal, J. M., trans. *The Śrīmad-Bhāgavatam*. 5 vols. 1929–39. Rpt. Calcutta: Oriental Publishing, 1952.

Sen, R. N., trans. *Brahma Vaivarta Purāṇa*. Sacred Books of the Hindus, no. 24. Allahabad: Panini Office, 1920–22.

Shastri, J. L. ed., Board of Scholars, trans. *Ancient Indian Tradition and Mythology Series*. 37 vols. to date. Vols. 1–4, *Śiva Purāṇa*. Vols. 5–6, *Liṅga Purāṇa*. Vols. 7–11, *Bhāgavata Purāṇa*. Vols. 12–14, *Garuḍa Purāṇa*. Vols. 15–19, *Nārada Purāṇa*. Vols. 20–21, *Kūrma Purāṇa*. Vols. 22–26, *Brahmāṇḍa Purāṇa*. Vols. 27–30, *Agni Purāṇa*. Vols. 31–32, *Vārāha Purāṇa*. Vols. 33–36, *Brahma Purāṇa*. Vol. 37, *Vāyu Purāṇa*. Delhi: Motilal Banarsidass, 1970-

Taluqdar of Oudh, trans. *Matsya Purāṇa*. Sacred Books of Hindus, no. 17. 1916–17. Rpt. Delhi: Oriental Publishers, 1972.

Wilson, Horace Hayman, trans. *The Viṣṇu Purāṇa*. 1840. Rpts. New York: B. Franklin, 1969. Calcutta: Punthi Pustak, 1972.

See also translated excerpts from the Purāṇas in "Anthologies of Texts," under "General Sources."

Theism, Sectarianism, and Worship

Secondary Sources

Bhāndārkar, Sir Ramkrishna G. *Vaiṣṇavism, Śaivism and Minor Religious Systems*. 1913. Rpt. Varanasi, India: Indological Book House, 1965.

Bharati, Agehananda. *The Tantric Tradition*. Garden City, N.Y.: Doubleday, 1970.

Bhattacharyya, Narendra Nath. *Ancient Indian Rituals and Their Social Contents*. Delhi: Manohar Book Service, 1975.

Brahma, Nalini Kanda. *Philosophy of Hindu Sādhana*. London: Routledge & Kegan Paul, 1932.

Chatterji, J. C. *Kashmīr Śaivaism*. Albany, N.Y.: State University of New York Press, 1986.

Clothey, Fred W., and J. Bruce Long. *Experiencing Śiva: Encounter with a Hindu Deity*. Columbia, Mo.: South Asian Books, 1983.

Daniélou, Alain. *Hindu Polytheism*. New York: Pantheon Books, 1964.

Dasgupta, Shashibhusan. *Obscure Religious Cults*. Calcutta: Firma K. L. Mukhopadhyay, 1969.

Dhavamony, Mariasusai. *Love of God According to Śaiva Siddhānta*. Oxford: Clarendon Press, 1971.

Diehl, Carl Gustav. *Instrument and Purpose: Studies on Rites and Rituals in South India*. Lund, Sweden: Hakan Ohlssons, 1956.

Dimock, Edward C., Jr. *The Place of the Hidden Moon: Erotic Mysti-*

cism in the Vaiṣṇava-sahajiyā Cult of Bengal. Chicago: University of Chicago Press, 1966.

Dubois, Abbé J. A. *Hindu Manners, Customs and Ceremonies.* Translated by Henry K. Beauchamp. 3d ed. Oxford: Clarendon Press, 1906.

Eschmann, Anncharlotte, et al., eds. *The Cult of Jagannāth and the Regional Tradition of Orissā.* South Asia Institute, University of Heidelberg, South Asian Studies, no. 8. New Delhi: Manohar, 1978.

Gonda, Jan. *Aspects of Early Viṣṇuism.* 1954. Rpt. Delhi: Motilal Banarsidass, 1969.

———. *Viṣṇuism and Śivaism: A Comparison.* London: Athlone Press, 1970.

———. *Medieval Religious Literature in Sanskrit.* A History of Indian Literature, vol. 2, no. 1. Wiesbaden: Otto Harrassowitz, 1977.

Goudriaan, Teun, and Sanjukta Gupta. *Hindu Tantric and Śāktic Literature.* A History of Indian Literature, vol. 2, no. 2. Wiesbaden: Otto Harrassowitz, 1981.

Gupta, Sanjukta, et al. *Hindu Tantrism.* Handbuch der Orientalistik, vol. 2, no. 4. Leyden: E. J. Brill, 1979.

Kinsley, David R. *The Divine Player (A Study of the Kṛṣṇa-Līlā).* Delhi: Motilal Banarsidass, 1979.

Kramrish, Stella. *The Hindu Temple.* 2 vols. 1946. Rpt. Delhi: Motilal Banarsidass, 1976.

Lorenzen, David N. *The Kāpālikas and Kālāmukhas: Two Lost Śaivite Sects.* Australian National University, Centre of Oriental Studies, Oriental Monograph Series, no. 12. New Delhi: Thompson Press, 1972.

MacNicol, Nicol. *Indian Theism, From the Vedic to the Muhammadan Period.* 2d ed. Delhi: Munshiram Manoharlal, 1968.

Pandey, Raj Bali. *Hindu Saṃskāras.* 2d rev. ed. Delhi: Motilal Banarsidass, 1969.

Rao, T. A. Gopinatha. *Elements of Hindu Iconography.* 2 vols. 2d ed. New York: Paragon, 1968.

Sachau, Edward C., trans. *Alberunī's India.* 2 vols. in 1. 1910. Rpt. New Delhi: Oriental Books Reprint Corp., 1983.

Shivapadasundaram, S. *The Shaiva School of Hinduism.* London: Allen & Unwin, 1934.

Singer, Milton, ed. *Krishna: Myths, Rites and Attitudes.* Chicago: University of Chicago Press, 1968.

Stevenson, Margaret (Sinclair). *Rites of the Twice-Born*. 1920. Rpt. New Delhi: Oriental Books Reprint Corp., 1971.

Schulman, David Dean. *Tamil Temple Myths; Sacrifice and Divine Marriage in South Indian Śaiva Tradition*. Princeton: Princeton University Press, 1980.

Venkatachari, K. K. A. *The Maṇipravāla Literature of the Śrīvaiṣṇa Ācāryas: 12th to 15th Century A.D.* Ananthacharya Research Institute Series, no. 3. Bombay: The Institute, 1978.

Woodroffe, Sir John (Arthur Avalon). *Shakti and Shākta*. 2d ed. Madras: Genesh, 1929.

Yocum, Glenn E. *Hymns to the Dancing Śiva: A Study of Māṇikkavācakar's Tiruvācakam*. New Delhi: Heritage Publishers, 1982.

See also sections of works that deal with theism, sectarianism, and worship cited under "General Sources," and the appropriate sections in P. V. Kane, *History of Dharmaśāstra*.

Translated Texts

Hooper, J. S. M., trans. *Hymns of the Āḻvārs*. Calcutta: Association Press, 1929.

Kingsbury, F., and G. E. Phillips, trans. *Hymns of the Tamil Śaivite Saints*. London: Oxford University Press, 1921.

Pope, G. U., ed. and trans. *The Tiruvācagam or "Sacred Utterances" of the Tamil Poet, Saint and Sage Māṇikkavācagar*. Oxford: Clarendon Press, 1900.

Ramanujan, A. K., trans. *Speaking of Shiva*. Baltimore: Penguin Books, 1973.

———, trans. *Hymns of the Drowning: Poems for Viṣṇu by Nammāḻvār*. Princeton: Princeton University Press, 1981.

Rhodes Bailly, Constantia, trans. *Śaiva Devotional Songs of Kashmīr: A Translation and Study of Utpaladeva's Śivastotrāvalī*. SUNY Series in the Shaiva Traditions of Kashmir. Albany, N.Y.: State University of New York Press, 1987.

Zvelebil, K. V., trans. *The Lord of the Meeting Rivers: Devotional Poems of Basavaṇṇa*. Delhi: Motilal Banarsidass, 1984.

See also translated excerpts from the Purāṇas and other appropriate translations in the "Anthologies of Texts," under "General Sources."

Modern Hindu Movements

Secondary Sources

Choudhary, K. P. S. *Modern Hindu Mysticism*. Delhi: Motilal Banarsidass, 1981.

Farquhar, J. N. *Modern Religious Movements in India*. New York: Macmillan, 1924.

Isherwood, Christopher. *Ramakrishna and His Disciples*. New York: Simon & Schuster, 1965.

Iyengar, K. R. Srinivasa. *Śrī Aurobindo: A Biography and a History*. 2 vols. 3d ed. Pondicherry: Śrī Aurobindo Āshram, 1972.

Jayakar, Pupul. *Krishnamurti: A Biography*. San Francisco: Harper & Row, 1986.

McLeod, W. H. *Gurū Nānak and the Sikh Religion*. Oxford: Clarendon Press, 1968.

———. *Early Sikh Tradition: A Study of the Janamsākhīs*. Oxford: Clarendon Press, 1980.

Mukherjee, Dilip Kumar. *Chaitanya*. New Delhi: National Book Trust, 1970.

Nikhilānanda, Swāmī. *Vivekānanda: A Biography*. New York: Ramakrishna-Vivekananda Center, 1953.

Phillips, Stephen H. *Aurobindo's Philosophy of Brahman*. Leyden: E. J. Brill, 1986.

See also sections of works that deal with modern Hinduism cited under "General Sources."

Texts and Translations

Aurobindo, Śrī. *Śrī Aurobindo Birth Centenary Library*. 30 vols. Pondicherry: Śrī Aurobindo Āshram Trust, 1972.

Bhaktivedānta, Swāmī A. C. Prabhupāda. *The Teachings of Lord Chaitanya: A Treatise on Factual Spiritual Life*. New York: International Society for Krishna Consciousness, 1968.

———. *The Nectar of Devotion: The Complete Science of Bhakti Yoga*. New York: Bhaktivedanta Book Trust, 1970.

———. *The Perfection of Yoga*. New York: Bhaktivedanta Book Trust, 1973.

Krishnamurti, Jiddu. *The Collected Works of Krishnamurti*. New York: Harper & Row, 1980.

———. *Krishnamurti to Himself: His Last Journal.* London: Gollancz, 1987.
Maharishi Mahesh Yogi. *The Science of Being and Art of Living.* New York: Signet Books, 1969.
McDermott, Robert A., ed. *The Essential Aurobindo.* New York: Schocken Books, 1973.
Rāmakrishna, Śrī. *The Gospel of Śrī Rāmakrishṇa.* Translated by Swami Nikhlānanda. 1944. Rpt. Mylapore, India. Śrī Rāmakrishna Math, 1969.
Richards, Glyn, ed. *A Source-book of Modern Hinduism.* London: Curzon Press, 1985.
Vivekānanda, Swāmī. *Selections from Swāmī Vivekānanda.* Calcutta: Advaita Ashram, 1963.
———. *The Complete Works of Swāmī Vivekānanda.* Mayavati Memorial Edition. 8 vols. Calcutta: Advaita Ashram, 1965.
See also appropriate sections of works cited in "Anthologies of Texts," under "General Sources."

Reference Works

Dell, David, J., et al., eds. *Guide to Hindu Religion.* Boston: G. K. Hall, 1981.
Diehl, Katharine Smith. *Religions, Mythologies, Folklores: An Annotated Bibliography.* 2d ed. New York: Scarecrow Press, 1962.
Eliade, Mircea, ed. in chief. *The Encyclopedia of Religions.* 16 vols. New York: Macmillan, 1987.
Hastings, James, ed. *Encyclopaedia of Religion and Ethics.* 12 vols. plus index. New York: Scribner, 1908–27.
Holland, Barron, comp. *Popular Hinduism and Hindu Mythology: An Annotated Bibliography.* Westport, Conn.: Greenwood Press, 1979.
Liebert, Gösta. *Iconographic Dictionary of the Indian Religions.* Leyden: E. J. Brill, 1976.
Macdonell, Arthur A., and Arthur Berriedale Keith. *Vedic Index of Names and Subjects.* 2 vols. 1912. Rpt. Delhi: Motilal Banarsidass, 1967.
Mani, Vetta. *Purāṇic Encyclopaedia.* Delhi: Motilal Bannarsidass, 1975.
New Encyclopaedia Britannica. Macropaedia. 20 vols. 15th ed. Chicago: Encyclopaedia Britannica, 1974.

Stutley, Margaret, and James Stutley. *Harper's Dictionary of Hinduism*. New York: Harper & Row, 1977.

Walker, George Benjamin. *Hindu World: An Encyclopedic Survey of Hinduism*. New York: Praeger, 1968.

Index

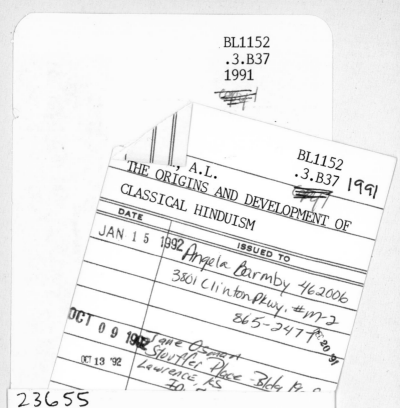